WHAT PEOPLE ARE SAYING

"Cheryl's work is honest, forthcoming, and ultimately, hopeful. She shares intimately her battles with her own mind, her therapists, and her eating disorder, but shows how persistence and commitment to self lead to true recovery. Not just stories, but clear outlines of recovery tools and lessons learned from each chapter, *Telling Ed No!* is educational, practical, and an inspiring story of triumph."

— **Kirsten Haglund, Miss America 2008**

"*Telling Ed No! and other practical tools to conquer your eating disorder and find freedom* is a raw, honest look at the harsh inner dialogue that goes on inside the mind of someone with an eating disorder. Cheryl Kerrigan poignantly illustrates the sharp contrast between the chains with which Ed enslaves and the freedom that Recovery gives. Like a trusted friend, Cheryl gently takes the reader's hand, persuasively encouraging a practical path toward healing, health, and wholeness."

— **Sari Fine Shepphird, PhD, Clinical psychologist and author of** *100 Questions and Answers about Anorexia Nervosa*

"Eating disorder survivor Cheryl Kerrigan shares her own day-by-day, step-by-step recovery journey in *Telling Ed No!* for one purpose—to prove to us that we can each be heroes in our own lives. When seen through Cheryl's eyes, asking for help becomes not a weakness but a unique source of strength. Cheryl also dedicates significant time to guiding us through techniques to tune out Ed's voice and tune in to a new, fresh, and powerful voice—the voice of recovery. *Telling Ed No!* is a timely and refreshing reminder that YES, doing the hard work of recovery really is worth it! Bravo, Cheryl!"

— **Shannon Cutts, Author of** *Beating Ana: How to Outsmart Your Eating Disorder and Take Your Life Back*

"*Telling Ed No!* is a must read for anyone struggling with an eating disorder. Cheryl's humor and honesty helps foster understanding and provides support to individuals as they face the real challenges of recovery. Her willingness and courage makes the journey feel less daunting and will help all feel supported and less alone."

- **Melissa Freizinger, PhD, Clinical Director, Laurel Hill Inn**

"Cheryl's vivid and candid portrayal of life with an eating disorder, what treatment is like, and what it takes to recover are helpful to those considering treatment. She also provides insightful questions to ponder throughout the book. She generously shares her painful struggles to help others recover. Great book!"

- **Jacquelyn Ekern, MS, LPC, Director, Eating Disorder Hope**

"Without providing triggering details (a rarity), Cheryl Kerrigan is able to share her journey of healing from an eating disorder and at the same time provide valuable, inspirational tips and tools for those who are ready to join her in *Telling Ed No!* As Cheryl's story attests, recovery does happen!"

Doris Smeltzer, MA, Authorn of *Andrea's Voice: Silenced by Bulimia*

"In *Telling Ed No!* Cheryl Kerrigan shares her personal story of her 22-year battle with an eating disorder, and how she managed to recover. Included in this book are real-life exercises and tools that she used to beat Ed (her eating disorder), showing us that recovery from an eating disorder really is possible. Ed's chains can be broken and you can take your life back. I highly recommend this book!"

Andrea Roe, Author of *You Are Not Alone—The Book of Companionship for Women with Eating Disorders*

Telling Ed No!

and other practical tools to conquer
your eating disorder and find freedom

CHERYL KERRIGAN

gürze books

Telling Ed No!
and Other Practical Tools to Conquer Your Eating Disorder and Find Freedom

© 2011 by Cheryl Kerrigan

Gürze Books
P.O. Box 2238
Carlsbad, CA 92018
760-434-7533
www.bulimia.com

Cover design by Rob Johnson, www.toprotype.com
Interior design by Abacus Graphics, Oceanside, CA, www.abacusgraphics.com

ISBN-13: 978-0-936077-62-8 (trade paperback)
978-0-936077-63-5 (e-pub)

Library of Congress Cataloging-in-Publication Data

Kerrigan, Cheryl, 1968-
Telling Ed no! : and other practical tools to conquer your eating disorder and find
freedom / Cheryl Kerrigan.
  p. cm.
 Summary: "Recovery from an eating disorder requires support of all kinds, and
this book is filled with ideas, exercises, and insights. Based on Kerrigan's own inspiring story, Telling Ed No! is a toolbox of over 100 practical recovery tools, from
family interventions, yoga, and massage, to music, role playing and even holding ice! Each tool brings the recovery process to life with prompts for reflection
and discussion. Readers looking for guidance will learn: why having a "treatment
team" is essential and how to assemble one, how to end self-destructive behaviors such as cutting and over-exercising, and how to transform Ed's controlling
rules into powerful, new recovery rules. Part-self-help book, part memoir, this
unique workbook combines the power of real-life experiences and candid straight
talk with suggestions and exercises that offer both hope and creative guidance"
-- Provided by publisher.
 ISBN 978-0-936077-62-8 (pbk.)
 1. Eating disorders--Popular works. I. Title.
 RC552.E18K47 2011
 616.85'2606--dc23
                        2011027824

NOTE:
The author and publisher of this book intend for this publication to provide accu-
rate information. It is sold with the understanding that it is meant to complement,
not substitute for, professional medical and/or psychological services.

3 5 7 9 0 8 6 4 2

For:

Amy
Bob
Dr. Gleysteen
Dr. Mollod
Thom
Walden Behavioral Care

With deep love and gratitude

CONTENTS

Section Three: Breaking The Chains—Separation And Strength

Section Four: The Escape—Finding Freedom

FOREWORD

Eating disorders are complicated. And they are painful—excruciatingly painful. Eating disorders are overwhelming and often lead people into the depths of discouragement, despair, and even hopelessness. They are clever; they are smart. If you have an eating disorder, it is actually smarter than you are. How strange is that? Yet you know that this is true. It outsmarts you at every turn. It manipulates you with shame, praise, insults, promises—whatever it takes to control your mind, your belief system, your relationships, your whole life. This is what an eating disorder will do: anything to remain in control. It never hesitates, never has a crisis of confidence, and never takes a day off. An eating disorder work ethic is incomparable.

Some people will tell you that eating disorders are not about food, but I disagree. Eating disorders are all about food: what to eat, what not to eat, when to eat, when not to eat, how to avoid food all together, how to eat massive amounts, how to get rid of the food that you do eat.

And some people will tell you that eating disorders are not really about your body, not really about your weight or size, or how you look in general. That, too, is not entirely true. How can it not be about these things when that is what your eating disorder talks to you about all day, every day?

A respected colleague of mine likes to tell her clients that "fat is not a feeling." Yet for many, "fat" is not only a feeling, it is the feeling that defines them.

But wait…

On the other hand, eating disorders are not about food. They are about desperate attempts to be in charge of something, about seeing yourself as different from everyone else, and not in a positive way. If you have an eating disorder, you probably suffer with relentless perfectionism, obsessions, compulsions, and what I have come to call "negative arrogance," believing yourself to be special, in that you are worse and/or more irreparable or hopeless than everyone else. "This book can probably help other people," you might think, "but probably not me."

But wait…

Eating disorders are not really about what you look like—your size or your weight. They are about feeling out of control of your own life and going to extreme measures to try to change this. They are about feeling like a freak, feeling trapped, seeing yourself as doomed to always fall short of who and what you should be.

And, of course, fat is not a feeling. Fat is a word used by people with eating disorders when they stop short of identifying the real feelings, the scary feelings below their experience of themselves as feeling fat. "I feel fat," is what you might say, instead of "I feel inadequate, ashamed, angry and deeply sad."

And, just in case you haven't noticed, eating disorders are full of paradox. They are about food, but they are not; about size and weight, but not; about feeling fat, but not really.

See what I mean? Eating disorders are complicated.

Recovery from eating disorders is simple.

I want to be crystal clear on this point: simple, but far from easy. In fact, recovery from your eating disorder may well be the hardest thing you will ever do. Recently, a client of mine who has battled both cancer and an eating disorder, told me that facing and overcoming her eating disorder has been far more difficult for her than treatment and recovery from cancer. This is what I said in response to that: wow.

Recovery is not for sissies. And there is, to my knowledge, no such thing as half-assed recovery. To overcome the control your eating disorder has over you, you must become determined and committed to do everything it will take to recover. There is no ordering recovery a la carte. No such thing as, "I'll have recovery but hold the weight gain," or "I'd like recovery with the meal plan on the side." Nope. You have to be all in.

* * *

Enter: Cheryl Kerrigan. In your hands you hold not just a book, but a box of excellent tools that, if you are willing to learn to use them, will help you to take your life back from your eating disorder. For some of you, the task may even be to take charge of your own life for the very first time. A tall order, no doubt, and that is why you need the help of people like Cheryl.

I will leave it for her to tell you about how and when we met. What I want you to know now, as you begin this book, is that you are in the capable hands of someone who is an inspirational leader, a compassionate teacher, and devoted advocate for you and everyone who has known the struggle and heartbreak wrought by eating disorders.

Cheryl will introduce you to my "separation metaphor," personifying your eating disorder as a unique entity that we have named "Ed," the acronym for eating disorder. To quote a lyric from Jenni Schaefer and Judy Rodman's song: "His name was Ed; he so controlled my head."* For Cheryl, this method of perceiving her disorder as a menacing internal force (named Ed), became the turning point she needed for her deepest healing to begin. She was a quick study when it came to understanding that recovery was not going to just happen, that if she wanted it, she was going to have to work for it. This point cannot be emphasized enough: understanding how your eating disorder came to be, and how it controls you, will not save you. Far too often, I see people—including treatment professionals—making that mistake. There is a big difference between becoming an expert on eating disorders and becoming an expert on eating disorder recovery. With *Telling Ed No!* Cheryl is going to help you to become the latter.

Be sure that your pen has plenty of ink; don't just read this book, use it. Mark in it, write notes in the margins. Keep a notebook handy, and do the exercises Cheryl describes. Really do them. If something shows even the slightest promise, then do it again, and again, and again. Cheryl is a smart woman, but that is not the main reason this book exists. The main reason is that she understands that smarts without action, theory without application, insight without follow-through, are all meaningless. Lessons from the best piano teacher do nothing to insure that I can play the piano. Recovery that stops at learning is not recovery. Recovery is about practice.

Eating disorders are complicated and painful. Recovery is simple—but hard, hard work. If you are looking for someone to show you the easy way out, you will have to look elsewhere. Cheryl will never tell you that this is easy, and neither will I. But if you have hurt enough, if you are sick and tired of being controlled by this intrapersonal control freak we call "Ed," then *Telling Ed No!* is your box of tools. Read on. Make notes. Discover what works best for you. Not just what makes sense, but what works.

Learn from Cheryl's story; use the heck out of the excellent tools that follow; when you make a mistake, correct it; when you lose your place, find it again; when you feel like giving up, don't. When Ed tells you, as he already has, that you are not going to be able to do this, stand up, lean toward him, look him straight in the eye and tell him No!

Thom Rutledge, LCSW
February 6, 2010
Nashville, Tennessee

*Life Without Ed, music and lyrics by Jenni Schaefer and Judy Rodman

INTRODUCTION

*I sit in a dark space, isolated from the world. I have only
one companion. When I try to speak, he degrades me.
When I try to run away, he catches me. When I try to be
happy, he forbids it. He controls my every move. His name
is Ed…and he is my eating disorder.*

My battle with toxic eating disorder thoughts began at age
five, progressed into anorexia in my teens, and continued
through my late thirties. I spent over 22 years as a captive of
this deadly disease until I found the strength to break free.

Based on my own recovery from an eating disorder, *Telling
Ed No!* brings the recovery process to life. It combines over
100 practical tools with real-life scenarios and shows you it
can be done. At the end of each chapter is a list that summa-
rizes the various tools, as well as a reflection section with questions and exercises to encourage journaling and discussion for
navigating your own path. You can read *Telling Ed No!* straight
through, or a section at a time to reflect on and practice each
tool and exercise that is offered.

A key to my healing journey was psychotherapist Thom
Rutledge's method of identifying the eating disorder as a destructive relationship with a person named Ed rather than a
condition. I have written *Telling Ed No!* using this perspective.
Note that I refer to my eating disorder as Ed during my early
life, as well; I've done this for the sake of clarity.

From the start of my recovery, I listened to and fought
Ed all the while not understanding that he was separate from
me. Even when I was trying my hardest to get better, I still felt

intertwined with Ed. It was only later, through my work with Thom, that I understood and was able to see my eating disorder as a separate entity, something I did not have to identify with, something I could actually learn to defy.

Up until that point, the battle in my head had been constant. Ed insisted that I do everything perfectly; Ed told me I was fat and ugly; and Ed told me what to eat, when to eat, and why. Ed had rules for me to follow in every situation. Obsessive thoughts about food, weight, calories, behaviors, and body image controlled every minute of every day because Ed came with me everywhere: to the playground, dance class, baton lessons, singing lessons, softball practice, color guard, school, work, and out with friends. He was always right beside me, whispering or yelling in my ear. He was my constant companion. He never let me down...or did he? Having Ed as my best friend and knowing I was never alone made me feel safe and secure, but the destructiveness he brought with him was hurting the very core of my being—my essence, my soul. Ed was dragging me down into a black hole and I was slowly dying.

However, after many unsuccessful attempts to break free from Ed, a time came when I was ready, with help, to make the commitment necessary. I also had the drive within me to do it. From a family intervention to life in a treatment center and beyond, *Telling Ed No!* shows my raw emotions, tough decisions, fears, and major triumphs while learning to incorporate food into my daily life in a healthy way. In writing it, I seek not only to relate the story of my recovery, but also to bring the light of hope to others lost in the darkness of this terrible disease. Recovery is possible and it can be achieved. Ed *can* be silenced.

While *Telling Ed No!* is filled with recovery tools for you to use in your journey, I also want to share with you five important forces that helped guide me to freedom so that you will be inspired.

First is my treatment team—Bob Bordonaro, Thom Rutledge, Amy Aubertin, Dr. Suzanne Gleysteen, and Dr. Daniel Mollod. Professional help is essential to recovery. My team held my hand every step of the way and kicked me in the butt when I needed it. They kept me motivated and picked me up when I fell. I have felt held, supported, understood, and comforted by every one of them. Without their support and guidance, I wouldn't be here today. I trust them (which was very hard to do), and I respect and love each one of them.

The second force that helped me the most was seeing (and hearing) the separation between Ed and me. It was a turning point—one of my "Aha!" moments. Through Thom Rutledge's intrapersonal therapy methods using exercises and role-playing, I was able to see and hear for the first time that I was not my eating disorder: Ed and I were separate entities. It was amazing. Finally realizing that I had something to fight against—rather than feeling like I was always fighting with myself—was instrumental in my healing process. Believe me when I tell you that you are NOT your eating disorder. (I go into more detail about Thom's work with me in Section Three).

The third force in my journey is the foundation on which I built my recovery: following my meal plan and nourishing myself. Without proper nutrition, the brain and body can't function properly, and Ed is always louder when you are deprived of nourishment. Giving your body the fuel it needs to think clearly is crucial. No matter how hard it was to take bite after bite, I knew I had to do it in order to continue the fight—and it worked.

Finally, the fourth and fifth vital forces in my recovery process have been patience and persistence. My treatment team told me that recovery is not a straight line, and boy, they were right. I fell down and got up many, many times, but most important, I learned each time. Also, recovery doesn't happen overnight; it's a process—one that I took to heart. I had to learn to be patient yet persistent in my quest for freedom. Slowing down and taking one meal, one feeling, even one moment at a time was hard, but necessary. Being persistent in *using* and *practicing* each tool (sometimes repeatedly) and never giving up on myself, or recovery, proved successful.

Recovery is hard work, but it is well worth everything you might go through to be free—to learn, to discover, to feel, to connect, to live. Just imagine being able to go out to eat and truly enjoy yourself; being free from the obsessive thoughts of calories, food, and behaviors; the freedom to exercise for the true pleasure of it; having a social life full of friends and family. All of these things are possible.

Everyone's path to recovery is different, but patience, practice, time, and commitment are necessities for survival. Take what you can from my story, use it in your own life, and leave the rest behind. Remember, you have the power and ability to get well. The choice is yours. Recovery *does* happen. Never give up and always believe. You are worth it and you deserve it. If I can do it, you can do it! Believe in yourself. I do!

SECTION 1

WHEN ED
HAD CONTROL

1

BORN INTO CAPTIVITY

"I was already tortured by bad body image, low self-esteem, and negative thoughts. I was five years old."

"Unique, Cheryl, you need to stay unique," Ed said.

From there, a life of imprisonment began.

I came into the world two and a half months early and weighed only three pounds. The doctors didn't think I would survive, but I did. From earliest memory, everyone around me let me know I had been born a preemie and was very small for my age. I even had a loving pet name, "my little three pounder." I heard that truth, but I wasn't the only one listening. Ed heard it too.

When I was young, everyone doted on me. I loved the attention and the recognition, which made me feel unique and special. Unfortunately, Ed took those feelings, along with my vulnerability, and twisted them together by telling me I could maintain that status only by doing what he said. He was beginning to lay down the rules, and if I wanted to be happy, loved, and special, I needed to obey them.

"Move next to your brother so I can take a picture. Smile! You look so pretty. You are going to make lots of new friends. I am so proud of you." These were all things my mom said to me when I was getting ready for my first day of kindergarten. Sadly, I could not feel the excitement or joy she was feeling. My thoughts were quite different.

I was thinking, *My feet are too big for my body. This dress makes me look puffy. Everyone will be staring at me. No one will like me!* I was nervous, confused, and scared because I did not know what to expect on this journey called "school." My mother was telling me one thing, and Ed was telling me another. I was already tortured by bad body image, low self-esteem, and negative thoughts. I was five years old.

Like many young girls my age, I took dance lessons. The studio was right down the street from our house, and my mom took me to class on Saturday mornings. Walking into the building each week, my heart raced, my body temperature rose, and negative thoughts would come rushing in.

I remember feeling exposed in my tights and leotard, especially when I turned around and saw parents and other kids looking at us through the large window in the wall. As the music began and the teacher gave instructions, the families would stare and point. I immediately felt that it was me they were picking out from the crowd, me they were laughing at. I felt so ashamed, nervous, and unloved that my head would drop and my body would cave in on itself to protect my heart and soul.

Even the floor-to-ceiling mirror judged me with taunts like, "You are so uncoordinated, Cheryl. You aren't as good as the other girls, and you aren't pretty." This was confusing because I liked dancing a lot, but the thoughts and feelings that came with it were so critical. I felt like I was being pulled in two directions, and I didn't know what to do or how to defend myself.

Our dance studio had a lot of students, and at the end of the year we held a big recital at the John Hancock Building in Boston. After the performance, my family took me to the back of the hall to get a picture taken. I was smiling from ear to ear because I had a fun time onstage showing the audience all my moves. Because Ed had expected it, I had danced in perfect harmony with the rest of my group. I was so proud of myself. After the pictures, we went back into the hall to watch the rest of the show.

There I was, bursting with pride, when my mother took out some candy bars and asked me if I wanted one. A feeling of disgust took over my entire body, and I looked her right in the eyes and said, "I can't eat that, it makes you fat!" At age six, my biggest decision should have been whether I wanted one—or both—of them. But I didn't touch either. Ed had control of what I did and said and he wouldn't let go. When he whispered, "No candy for you, young lady," I obeyed.

Wednesday, May 12th was a beautiful sunny day. I was in second grade, and I spent it laughing and playing with friends in my backyard. But in an instant my world was turned upside down.

An explosion burst from the second floor. Glass came crashing down onto the driveway below and flames shot out of an upstairs window. I screamed and ran into the house to get my mother. Both of us, with my brother in tow, were able to get out, run to the end of the driveway, and pull the firebox. Fire trucks came and neighbors gathered around to watch fire and water engulf my home. I stood there shaking and crying, clinging to my mother in disbelief. Then fear set in. Questions flooded my mind as the life I knew went up in flames: What will happen to us now? Where will we live? What will I wear? Where will I sleep?

For a while, my family lived with relatives, but eventually we moved to a different city where I was enrolled in a new school, leaving behind the only life I had known. I felt lost, alone, and afraid. I often had nightmares about the fire and could still smell the smoke every time I closed my eyes.

Even though my surroundings were now completely different, I did have one constant—Ed. He was my best friend. "I'll take care of you," he said. "Don't be afraid." Ed made me feel comforted and secure. He told me that if I did what he said, new friends would find me and school would be great. "You will be happy and I will protect you if you only eat what I tell you to," he said. "Stay away from the bad foods and you will stay small and everyone will love you." So I listened and followed his lead. Little did I know that Ed wasn't a very good friend.

Later on I took baton in grammar school and had individual, duet, and group lessons. I enjoyed the challenge of learning new tricks and getting them perfect; I always strived to do everything perfectly. I felt compelled to get *every* trick and *every* routine down without a mistake and would practice for hours to be sure I was doing them right.

It was during group lessons and competitions, that I first found myself becoming obsessed with comparing my body to others. Puberty was around the corner, and my psyche was in tune with that fact. I judged myself by what others looked like and "sized myself up" accordingly. Sadness set in when I realized I did not look like everyone else, always wishing I was thinner, taller, and prettier.

The competitions, which were hard enough on my self-esteem, were made even worse by the fact that they included a modeling category. We had to wear gowns and parade around like beauty queens. I never won, which reinforced my feelings of being the fattest, ugliest girl there. I tried to compensate by practicing more—which in turn made me beat myself up when I did not reach the perfection Ed told me I should. I felt like a failure—a loser right down to the core of my being.

My baton group also participated in the town's Halloween parade. My uniform consisted of a short white skirt and jacket over a red leotard with a black cummerbund. Every year I prayed I would not have to order a new skirt or cummerbund because that would mean I had gotten fatter. That fear consumed me. Alone in my room, I would get out my old uniform and pull the skirt up to my waist to see if it fit. As I brought the clasp together to see if it would close, I saw flashes of people laughing and pointing at me. The next moment was crucial: Would I feel embarrassed, or would I feel relieved? Ed was ready to give me directions no matter what the outcome.

Ed has subtle ways of grabbing our attention. Sometimes he uses clothing as way to measure our failure or success. He deems us perfect if we fit into the mold he creates. I believed him and used that cummerbund to assess my body. Only if it fit on the third snap—the smallest—would pride fill my chest and my lips turn up in a smile, because it meant I had "succeeded."

REFLECTIONS

Looking back, what are some of your earliest memories of disordered thoughts and/or behaviors related to food and your body? How did Ed grab your attention? What age were you? Was it a gradual progression?

2

ME + ED = NORMAL

"I desperately wanted to be smaller and thinner than all the other girls. I thought I needed to be that way in order to be loved and stay unique. Ed told me so, and I believed him."

As it does for many adolescents, puberty brought with it intensely negative feelings about my body. But for someone who was already in Ed's grasp, these feelings were more intense and more destructive. My negative body image worsened, and my eating disorder behaviors became more entrenched. I constantly compared myself to and competed with everything and everyone—including myself. I was aware of what other people around me were eating and doing, and I became increasingly obsessed with calories and fat content. As usual, Ed was telling me what, when, and how to eat, and his voice was growing more dominant and much louder. He told me to increase my exercise, stick to a rigid schedule, monitor my weight, and to do it all perfectly. I did what he said as I did *not* want to disappoint him.

When middle school came, my body began to change rapidly. It felt out of control, and I wanted to stay small! *I need to make it stop...stop getting bigger. It is ruining everything!* Just walking the halls at school made me feel insecure in my own skin. I desperately wanted to be smaller and thinner than all the other girls. I thought I *needed* to be that way in order to be loved and stay unique. Ed told me so, and I believed him. It was all I knew; it was my "normal."

I became hyperaware of what was going into my mouth

and how the food was disfiguring my body—or so I thought. (Now I know that I had symptoms of body dysmorphic disorder (BDD), which caused me to believe that I could see my physical changes right before my eyes whenever I ate.) Every bite felt like a shard of glass going down my throat, and when it rested inside, it felt as heavy as cement and as big as an elephant. The disfigurement I "saw" all over disgusted me. I needed to smooth out all the fat and make it look thin again!

My friendships were also being tested, and schoolwork was becoming more difficult. I felt overwhelmed, lost, and alone. I was trying to figure out who I was, which clique I wanted to join, what I should wear to fit in, and which activities I should do. The peer pressure was intense. Although I was afraid of being banished and alone if I chose the wrong direction, Ed told me not to worry. "Just listen to me and you'll be fine. I know what's best for you. I won't let you down," he would say. "Be thin and you'll be accepted, happy, and as special as you were when you were younger." He promised that I would be popular and smart as long as I did what he said, when he said to do it. So I listened.

During this time, my low self-esteem and poor body image were rampant. Feeling ugly, fat, and worthless, I increasingly turned to disordered behaviors to compensate. My younger brother was a model, and his face filled the pages of catalogs, magazines, TV commercials, and game covers. I accompanied him and my mother on photo shoots, secretly wishing I was pretty and thin enough to partake in all the glamour. It never happened.

Throughout my high school years, Ed came with me to choir practice, singing lessons, drama, and color guard. He was beside me at every test I took and during every homework assignment I finished. I had rules to follow. I needed to strive for perfection by getting straight A's, I needed to be the best in every activity I did, I needed to be a loyal friend and daughter all while restricting my intake and listening closely to Ed and his directions. I could not disobey. If I did, I felt like a disappointment—and that was not an option. I had to prove I was good at following the rules. I wanted Ed to be proud of me, to know that I was working hard. I did *not* want to fail.

Ed told me that certain foods were restricted and others were on the "bad list." Having those "bad" foods would make me a weak person and would only make me fatter. I had to stick with his "safe" foods in order to feel happy and safe. My behaviors and rituals around mealtimes were easy to hide because Ed taught me how. The better I became at completing my behaviors and rituals, the better I felt about myself. I was a master of disguise, and no one knew or caught on, which made me feel confident. I really believed that I looked and acted fine.

As time went by, though, things got worse. My weight continued to drop, my behaviors were dominating my life, my health was affected, my moods were up and down, and I began cutting myself to cope with daily stresses. Finally, I couldn't hide any longer. My parents began to comment about my weight and behaviors. Then my doctor caught on, and in my late teens, I was diagnosed with anorexia nervosa. She gave me suggestions and tips to help "break the cycle" and "get back on track," but she didn't closely watch my progress, which made me think I didn't really have a problem. This gave me permission to keep living the way I had been. After all, it was all I knew—my "normal."

REFLECTIONS

You might think that the rituals and behaviors of your daily life are "normal," but whose normal are they? They may look and feel normal to you, but upon reflection could they really be coming from Ed? Is he telling you to do them, is he giving you direction?

Also, what triggers your eating disorder and throws your behaviors into high gear? Is it emotional, physical, or social factors, or a combination of all three? Write down three scenarios where you find yourself turning to Ed for comfort and list the behaviors and rituals he instructs you to do.

3

PRISONER FOR LIFE?

"No matter what was going on, I ran to Ed for help and guidance—what to do, when to do it, and why. He was my security, embedded into my brain and built into my daily life—every minute of it."

When I was 18, I left for school in Boston having been accepted into a one-year, advanced business secretarial program. I was excited to get started on this next chapter of my life. I wish I could say I went alone, but Ed walked through the doors with me on the first day of school and never left my side. Because of my need to be the "perfect" student, feelings of stress, panic, anxiety, and fear surfaced early. To compensate, my self-injury and restricting behaviors worsened. And although Ed's rules for me became even more harsh, I didn't waiver.

Not only was I in an advanced program at school, I was also a member of Blessed Sacrament—a world-class Winter Guard. Winter Guard is a color guard activity performed indoors at a gym or arena during the winter months. The routines are performed to music and utilize various types of equipment (flag, rifle, saber), props, and dance moves. Spinning a rifle was a passion and talent I had picked up in high school. We practiced three days a week and had competitions on weekends. Ed liked this because it involved a lot of exercise, which, at this point in time, was becoming more dominant. I usually did my homework when I got home from practice at 11 p.m. at night. Then I was up at 5:30 a.m. to get ready and grab the train to school. Over and over this routine played out, while my health declined on Ed's short leash.

Turns out, Ed was my go-to method for dealing with every

emotion, hardship, *and* triumph. If I was happy, I ran and told Ed. He told me, "Great job, Cheryl, but tomorrow you need to listen to me more closely and your day will be even better." If I was sad, I ran to Ed and he told me, "It's okay Cheryl, I'll make you feel better. I'll fix it." No matter what was going on, I ran to Ed for help and guidance—what to do, when to do it, and why. He was my security, embedded into my brain and built into my daily life—every minute of it.

At this point, school was done and I had a new doctor who expressed her concern and gave me the name of a therapist to talk to about what was going on in my life. Although I went to the appointments and talked about my thoughts and feelings, I had difficulty admitting I had a problem. I didn't see that there was anything wrong with the way I was living. It was just me, and that's the way it was; it was my "normal."

As time went on, I got a job, got married, and built a new house—all with Ed at my side. When Winter Guard ended (at that time you could only march until a certain age, and I had reached it), I took up singing in a local adult choir where I had joined the board and then became the group's president. Ed led me to believe that the only reason good things were happening in my life was because I was listening to his advice.

Although things looked great on the outside, Ed was wearing me down so much on the inside that I needed a higher level of care. My therapist suggested a treatment facility. By this time I was 29 years old and Ed had taken over. My health was compromised, I couldn't concentrate, my body was giving out, and I was depressed. I had to leave my post as choir president and leave my group. I was also faced with telling my boss of 11 years about my eating disorder because I had to take a leave of absence from my job. I was the company's assistant treasurer, responsible for over $150 million! I was sure *I* was in control—but in reality, Ed was.

It was my first hospitalization in an eating disorder facility, and I was scared. I did not know what to expect nor did I want to let go of my best friend. I had known Ed for so long! Also, his voice was louder than ever in the hospital because he did not like the fact that I was in weight restoration mode, doing what the staff asked. He ranted that they didn't know what they were talking about and that they didn't know me like *he* did. He assured me that they were lying and only wanted me to get fat. He told me that I didn't have a problem and that I wasn't sick anyway. In fear of being viewed unwilling and a less-than-perfect patient, I participated in groups and ate according to my prescribed meal plan. Although I was proud of myself for taking these steps, I was not too convinced that I wanted to be without Ed forever. Forever is a long time.

When I was released from the hospital, I continued to work on my recovery by sticking to my meal plan and going to all my outpatient appointments. Even though I was still unsure about the process, I was doing it anyway.

Then, three months after I got out of the hospital, one of my best friends suddenly passed away. I was devastated—lonely, sad, and angry. Rather than running to my family and friends for support, though, I turned to Ed to help me feel safe, held, and comforted. In his negative behaviors, rules, and rituals, I found a (false) sense of control and normalcy, and things quickly went from bad to worse.

Eventually, I relapsed and ended up back in the hospital. I felt like such a failure, and my family and friends seemed so disappointed. They had hoped that I was "fixed" and "all better" and did not understand why it was not as simple as telling myself to "just eat." How I hated those words! An eating disorder is not only about food, but people who haven't suffered with one (or known someone who has) often don't understand that.

When I was discharged from the hospital for the second time, I was at a healthier weight, but my mind and thoughts were still in eating-disorder mode. Again, I had done what I was told in the hospital (and did it perfectly, I might add), but at my core, I was not committed to recovery. It seemed to be so much work and so much to learn, and the enormity of the task was paralyzing.

Years went by; a divorce happened, and another new life began. Ed, as always, remained a constant. No matter what I was going through, I could count on him. His voice was relentless, manipulative, and loud. What I didn't realize was that he didn't really care about me. My negative behaviors continued, and my mood went up and down along with my weight. I was back to living life with an eating disorder. It was my "normal," but that didn't make it right.

At this point, I was remarried to a wonderful woman and my job was going strong, although Ed seized every opportunity to remind me who was really in control. I still felt like something was missing, though, and I decided to go back to school at night to get my bachelor's degree. Another journey began, and with it came more stress, more self-criticism, more perfectionism, and more rules. So at age 33, I became the perfect student again and would not accept anything less than all A's. Ed was in my book bag, telling me what to eat, what not to eat, what to say, where to go, what to do, whom to do it with, and why. I also began comparing my body, my accomplishments (or lack there of), and my academics with my classmates.

My brain never shut off. I was constantly thinking about food, calories, rules, and behaviors, all while trying to concentrate on school and work. It was draining. I was also still self-injuring to try to cope with it all. The more negative behaviors I practiced, the better I felt—or so I thought. Even though I felt like "I" was in control, Ed was.

Years went by on autopilot. Even though I was married, and had friends and a job, I felt unfulfilled, empty, and alone. I couldn't understand why, because I was listening to Ed and doing everything he said to do. But my behaviors were out of control, my weight was at its lowest ever, and my health was failing. My days consisted of going to work and coming home to be alone with Ed. He wanted me all for himself, so I isolated myself and disengaged from friends and family. He dominated every thought, every situation, every feeling. I was in complete denial—a prisoner in my own life. Until one day…

Is Ed dominant in your life? Write down what he is telling you right now. When and how often does he show up throughout your day? Is he louder in the morning, at night, at work, at school, or at home?

SECTION 2

GAINING THE UPPER HAND

4

THE INTERVENTION

"Like a flash of lightning—clarity just for one split second—I realized I didn't want to live like this anymore. My family was right. My eating disorder was killing me, and I needed help to get better."

The nightly news was on TV as I dragged my frail, exhausted body across the kitchen to put our dirty dinner dishes in the sink. I was at my lowest weight ever, depressed and isolated from everyone except Ed. I was cleaning off my plate when the doorbell rang. That seemed odd because it was a Thursday night and we were not expecting company. Dread came over me; the thought of seeing or entertaining someone was just too much to bear. "Who the heck is that?" I said. My spouse, Rachel, answered the door, and in walked my brother and father. They looked so serious!

Instantly, my stomach started doing flips. Scary and horrible thoughts came to my mind as panic set in. *Someone is sick and dying and they have come to break the news. Who was it? Who was sick? Was it my nephew? My niece? Who? Someone say something!* I was frantic. I needed to know what was happening!

"What are you doing here? Is everything okay?" I asked, desperation in my voice.

"Sit down, Cheryl. We need to talk," they answered. So we all took seats at the kitchen table. The TV was turned off, and silence filled the room. There I sat, with people I loved, and I had nothing but fear running through my veins. *What is happening?* It felt like my life was about to change, and I did not know if it would be for the better or the worse. I was terrified.

For a moment, they all stared at me with a look of concern and then began firing away: "Cheryl, we love you and we are worried about you. You are very sick. You are withering away. You have anorexia. You need to get help NOW."

Their lips were moving, and I heard the words come out of their mouths, but it took me a minute to realize what was happening. This was an intervention! *You've got to be kidding me!* Shock, then anger enveloped me. I was practically shaking from all the adrenalin.

I yelled back, "I'm fine. You don't know what you're talking about! I'm functioning perfectly fine!" "I have friends, I have a job; I'm *fine!*"

Rachel replied, "Cheryl, you are *not* fine. You need help to get better. You need to go into treatment."

"No, I don't!"

Then my brother said, "Cheryl, your eating disorder is even beginning to affect my kids, and I can't let that happen anymore." I was stunned. *Did he just say I can't see his kids unless I get help?* Grief swept over me, and I started to cry. The thought of not being able to see or be with my niece and nephew was devastating. My heart felt like it was being ripped out of my body and thrown onto the floor.

Even as Rachel, my dad, and my brother continued talking, I could also hear Ed's voice shouting that they were blowing things out of proportion. He told me to just sit there and listen, and that they would be out of there in no time and things would get back to "normal." But what was normal? Were obsessing about food and weight, eating-disordered behaviors, triggers, bad body image, isolation, cutting myself, and depression the normal I really wanted?

The intervention dragged on for over an hour. It was exhausting. When everyone finally finished expressing their feelings, they each gave me a hug and told me they loved me. Rachel walked my dad and brother to the door, leaving me at the kitchen table. I could not move. My body felt like I had just run a marathon. My eyes were swollen shut from all the tears, and I felt hollow and empty inside. I had no fight left. With my last ounce of energy, I got up from the table, shaking with emotion, and went into the darkened living room—alone.

Sitting on the sofa with my arms wrapped around my knees, I cried while I rocked back and forth and wondered what to do. *I can't go into treatment; I don't have time; I will lose my job; I can't leave my family and friends.* The doubts and excuses went back and forth. Ed was saying one thing, and my family was saying the opposite. *Whom should I believe? What should I do?* I was so confused. I went to bed that night with a heavy heart and a head full of questions. I still had not come to any decisions when my eyes closed for the night.

The next morning, I woke up with a splitting headache. My body felt like it had been hit by a truck. I was happy it was Friday, but uncertain what events would play out in the days ahead. I went about my morning routine and left for work. The office was empty and quiet when I arrived, so I took a seat at my desk, stared at my computer, and just thought—about everything and everyone: where I had been, where I wanted to go, and what I wanted to become. I was petrified. I wanted to make the right decision, but was unsure of what that was. I felt alone and confused. With a heavy heart I said out loud, "Oh God, what should I do?"

Forty-five minutes of more agony passed, my emotions careening from fear to loneliness to panic, and then it happened. Like a flash of lightning—clarity just for one split second—I realized I didn't want to live like this anymore. My family was right. My eating disorder was killing me, and I needed help to get better.

I had come to a decision. I thought, *I better hurry and do it before Ed overpowers me and I change my mind!* So I got up from my desk, walked into a spare office, closed the door, and picked up the phone. My heart was beating out of my chest, and my hands were sweating so much that I had a hard time holding the receiver. It took me 15 minutes to finally dial the number because Ed kept trying to talk me out of calling. He was telling me that I was not sick enough to get help, that I was too fat to go to treatment, that my family and friends did not know what they were talking about. I could feel myself weakening, when, before I knew what was happening, someone said, "hello" on the other end of the line.

As I stumbled for the right words to say, I broke down. Sobbing, I told the woman on the phone, "I need help." She calmed me down and told me she was glad I had called and that she would do everything she could to help me. We talked for a while and her words of encouragement made me feel held, safe, and warm. I had made a connection. I thought, *I can do this; I will be okay.* I felt strong, alive, and scared all at the same time. When we hung up, I had an intake interview for the following Monday. *Get ready recovery, here I come!*

RECOVERY TOOLS

- Asking for help
- Trust

REFLECTIONS

Trusting someone other than Ed is vital to your recovery. Have any of your loved ones expressed concern for your health? We all need help seeing things from a healthy point of view—not Ed's. Think about people in your life that you trust. Whom will you trust to help rid you of your eating disorder—a family member, doctor, friend? Take the first step and reach out to them.

5

THE TREATMENT FACILITY

"Even though Ed was loud, obnoxious and yelling at me the entire time, I knew I was taking critical steps toward recovery just by participating."

I woke on Monday morning with my stomach in a knot. Even though I was cozy warm in my bed, I also had chills of uncertainty and fear. *Am I strong enough? Can I really do this?*

The sun was shining through my bedroom window as I rummaged through my drawers and piled clothes into my big black suitcase. I had no idea of what was ahead, and that thought was terrifying. But Rachel was there with hugs. She told me she was proud of me.

When it was time to leave, we tossed my bag into the back of our SUV and jumped inside. Pulling away from the house on that beautiful spring day, I turned to get one last look. Behind the holly bush and through the lilacs, I could see my dogs in the window, ever hopeful. Sadness washed through me. *When would I see them again?*

Rachel and I drove in silence. I remember cherishing our last few moments together as we pulled up to the building. Walden Behavioral Care (Walden) was in a five-story building made of stone and brick, which also housed a walk-in clinic, doctors' offices, and a children's hospital. Staff members were drinking coffee and milling around outside. I wondered if this solid-looking structure would become my home for a while, and if it held the key to my new life—a life of freedom. I'd find out after today's appointment.

We walked in together, bag in tow, and I briefly wondered

which of the four programs they would recommend for me, if any: inpatient treatment, partial hospitalization, intensive outpatient and residential treatment. The intake appointment would determine what type of care I needed.

On the way up to the fifth floor, my chin and lips were trembling with fear. We stepped off the elevator into the waiting room of what looked like a locked unit, and I picked up a phone on the wall to check in. Then Rachel and I settled into a couple of the oversized chairs to wait. Ed started in immediately: "What are you, stupid? What are you *doing?*" My eyes filled with hot tears.

It seemed like hours passed—although it was really only minutes—when a nurse opened the door to say they were ready for me. I was scared, but determined to approach the intake appointment with both an open heart and an open mind. I gave Rachel a hug goodbye then walked through the doors into the unknown.

Then the nurse led me to a "family room" with a big, fluffy, maroon sofa and green wing chairs. The window was open, and the fresh air was soothing.

When the doctor came in, I instantly tensed up. *What is he going to ask me? Am I going to get into the program? Will I have to eat in front of him?* My head was a cyclone of thoughts. He was tall with short brown hair, a beard, and glasses and he greeted me with a soft handshake and a reassuring smile. I could feel myself relax a little.

"Cheryl, how are you doing? Do you need anything?" he asked. Then he added, "I'm glad you're here." He seemed kind, and he had a calm yet confident demeanor that made me believe he would take care of me.

He sat down and began the interview. It was question after question and I concentrated hard on my answers. He wanted to know: what types of behaviors I had, what I consumed in a day, did I sleep through the night, did I self-injure, did I want to hurt myself, what was my family and health history, and so forth. He carefully wrote down my responses. I was sitting across from him like a scared little kid who didn't know if she was doing good or bad, and my nerves came back. They had me going so much that my leg started shaking and I began to fidget.

Finally, the interview ended. I was sent to the lab for blood work and then back to the family room to wait. I paced, not knowing if I was in or out. All the while Ed was firing away with the usual chatter about how stupid I was and how I didn't know what I was doing. "Just walk out now and go home," he said. "It won't work! Don't do it, Cheryl!"

The appointment had lasted a total of two hours, and I had two more to go before I found out what was ahead of me. So far, the process had been exhausting, and to have revealed so much was humiliating at times. But even though I could still hear Ed talking, I had pushed through, because I knew it was the only way to begin to heal.

When the doctor came back into the room he said, "Cheryl, because of your anorexia and your current behavior and medical status, we are admitting you into our inpatient program. Let's show you to your room," I shed tears of relief and gratitude. At that moment I knew I was not going to die from this disorder. I had been given hope, and I took it with open arms. I was not sure what would happen next, but I was sure about one thing: I was on my way to recovery, whatever that meant.

I was admitted to the inpatient unit. My new home was behind locked doors with 24-hour care, and 100 percent of my time would be structured. I was there to get medically stable, concentrate on myself, and begin the recovery process. I was being given another chance at life, and I was taking it.

I was put in Room #3 with a roommate. The furnishings were minimal—two twin beds, two bedside tables, and four chairs. I cautiously began unpacking my bag. I had brought pictures of Rachel, my dogs, and my niece and nephew, along with my stuffed cow, Moo Moo, arts-and-crafts supplies, a book, a DVD player, my iPod, and my journal. As I set these things out, I was thinking about how much I was hoping to find the bigger pieces of myself, those without Ed. I knew I had a tough fight ahead, because he was right there reminding me that I was doing everything wrong, and that these people didn't know me like he did.

Being away from my home and family was tough enough, but I also faced something even more difficult, the one thing I hated most—eating. The dining room held about 25 people and had three large tables, two refrigerators, a microwave, cabinets, and a sink. One side of the room had a wall of windows with a view of Boston in the distance. There were plants and flowers on the windowsill, and affirmations like "Believe in Yourself," "You Can Do It," and "Stay Strong" all over the walls and ceiling. There were also questions and recovery topics taped to the wall to promote reflection and discussion, and music played in the background.

My first meal was agonizing, and I cried with each bite I took. I felt guilty, like I was doing something wrong by eating. My hands shook and I had tears in my eyes as each piece of food passed by my lips. It was torture. Of course Ed was chatting in my ear the entire time, telling me I did not need to be here and that I was going about this all wrong. The anxiety was overwhelming. My only solace was that I was surrounded by people just like me, and I felt comforted knowing I wasn't alone.

I awoke the next morning to a bright spring day. The sun from my window hit my skin and warmed me all over. I stood in line for the bathroom, then got the corner shower—the one with windows and sunlight coming through! I dared to hope. *Is this a sign of things to come?* I felt ready.

Dr. P., the psychiatrist, came and got me for our first meeting. He looked to be in his late 30s or early 40s, and had dark hair and a soft voice. He started the session by asking a few routine questions. Then he asked about my behaviors and thoughts. I was open and honest with my answers because I wanted recovery and I trusted that I was in a safe place that could help me.

Dr. P. told me about medication that could calm down my racing thoughts and fight my depression. I never liked to take pills, and having to rely on them seemed like a failure to me. But I knew that my mind was constantly on the go. I obsessed about everything from the weather, to food, to the rituals of my disorder. It was exhausting to always have a mind that was going, going, going. I could hardly sleep at night because it would not stop. So I decided to try the medication—anything to slow down my racing thoughts.

Next, I moved on to a meeting with a nutritionist whose name was Lindsey. A young woman in her late twenties or so, she had long, dark hair, a great smile, and a calm and friendly personality that got me through the excruciating process of talking about meal plans. During our discussion I laid bare all my anxiety and fear, often in tears as certain foods and amounts were brought into the conversation. When we finally had a plan in place (which Ed was ticked off about), I was confident about being able to follow through with it.

Dr. B., the medical doctor, did a quick checkup, looked at my lab work, and asked about any concerns I had regarding my health. Routine EKGs were scheduled and done right in my room. Anything I needed or worried about was being taken care of for me.

Finally, it was time for me to meet with my social worker. I was in the group room when a man I didn't recognize walked in and asked me to come with him. When we were outside in the hall, he turned and said, "Hi, Cheryl. I'm Bob, your social worker. Let's go to your room and talk." I walked down the hall with my eyes wide and my gaze pinned to the floor. My first thoughts were: *There is no way I will be able to talk to a guy. This will be totally useless. I came here for this?* I was angry and disappointed. I imagined that fear would make my walls go up, and I wouldn't be able to relate to a male therapist.

Bob was tall with dark hair and wore glasses. We got to my room and closed the door behind us. He reintroduced himself and began to talk. I had no idea what to expect or how I would react to all of this. Despite my negativity, I reminded myself why I was there. I listened intently to what he said, and to my surprise, I liked him. I could tell he knew his stuff and, most important, that he actually understood my craziness.

"Do you want to get better?" he asked.

"Yes, that's why I'm here," I replied.

"Tell me the types of things you are hearing in your head," he said.

I was hesitant to answer this at first for fear I would sound like an idiot, but I knew I had to press on or my recovery would never happen.

"I am being told that I do not deserve to be here," I said, "that I am not sick enough to be here, that you do not know what you are talking about, and that I should not trust you." I also told him about the racing thoughts I was having about calories and food.

He listened to me without judgment, and then we talked. He assured me that I was not crazy and that he understood. He was compassionate, honest, and up front, and I was actually comfortable talking with him. By the end of our session, I realized that I needed and really wanted him to be on my side through my recovery process. For the rest of the day, I couldn't stop thinking about the fact that I had actually connected with a male therapist. I was shocked!

Days came and went with one meal and snack after another. The refeeding process was tremendously difficult for me because I had to trust the process, trust the food and trust my body—not something I was accustomed to. But I had to start somewhere. Ed grew angrier each day, belittling me and telling me I was stupid and getting fatter with every bite: "You don't know what you are doing, Cheryl. You are ruining everything we've worked for."

Loud as Ed was, my sessions with Bob and Lindsey and the groups were all helping. I was learning some new skills and tools to support my recovery, like thought stopping, affirmations, journaling, arts and crafts, expressive movement, peer support and yoga. The big question was, would I be able to put them to use outside of this cocoon? Being in treatment was difficult and arduous, but it was also safe because everyone around me knew how and what I was feeling at any given moment. The outside world was not like this.

During my stay, I was fortunate to have a steady stream of visits from friends and family. I was never without support. My dad came to see me every night, always asking how my day had been, how I had done with the food, and how I felt about it. And he encouraged me by telling me he loved me and by saying, "Stay strong, honey. You can do it."

Friends came to see me and we sat in my room, crowded around my bed, and chatted about the daily goings-on. I loved hearing about what went on at work, the latest family dramas, and their plans for the upcoming days. It helped to occupy my mind with something other than all the eating and feeling I was doing day in and day out. They also brought me fun arts-and-crafts projects, which gave me something to do right after meals—and helped take my mind off the food I had just eaten. These times were an invaluable support for my recovery.

Art and dance therapy were also provided, both of which were very interesting and new to me. These groups forced me to notice many difficult and uncomfortable feelings that were part of my eating disorder, like my insecurity, self-judgment, low self-esteem, fear, and anxiety. My heart and mind would race, my insides would shake, and I would feel exposed—like I had when I was little. But bringing those feelings to the surface and utilizing dance and art to work through them was truly liberating. I also got to experience using a positive behavior rather than a negative one. A revelation!

The nutrition groups were key as well. They taught me how my body reacts to certain foods and what I needed for proper function. For instance, learning that oils benefit my brain helped me when I struggled to eat them. I tried to focus on the fact there would only be benefits to adding a variety of new foods to my diet.

Don't get me wrong, I was skeptical about all of these experiences, especially because Ed told me to be, but I took notes, and kept my mind and heart open. Even though Ed was loud and obnoxious and was yelling at me the entire time, I knew I was taking critical steps toward recovery just by participating.

RECOVERY TOOLS

- Inpatient treatment
- An open mind and heart
- Arts and crafts
- Talking with friends

- Support groups
- Talk therapy
- Affirmations
- Music
- Journaling
- Reading
- Expressive therapy (dance and art)
- Nutritional therapy
- Family
- Friends
- Following a meal plan
- Honesty
- Trust

REFLECTIONS

Have you ever thought about entering treatment? What's stopping you? Write down some ideas about what may be holding you back from accepting professional help. Is Ed telling you not to go? Don't believe him! Push the fear and Ed aside and write down what you would hope to get out of treatment.

6

LET PEOPLE IN

"I was blessed to have these individuals touch my life. Each one gave me something that I was able to take with me and use in my recovery and they all have a special place in my heart"

While you are in treatment, you are away from your friends and family in a place that is difficult, uncomfortable, scary, hopeful, and exciting all at once. You are vulnerable as you put your self into the hands of people you do not know. You may ask yourself, "Am I safe? Will these people really help? Are they even *nice?*" For me, the answer to all these questions was a resounding, "Yes!"

It was pretty evident from the moment I walked into Walden that the staff was there to help me get better. They treated me like I was a human being, not a disease. They showed me respect and expected respect in return. They understood that all the inpatients were doing the one thing that scared us the most—eating. They did not downplay that fact and were extremely supportive.

There were many staff members I looked forward to seeing every day to help me get through the pain I was dealing with. These individuals put a smile on my face and reminded me what I was working toward *and* what I was leaving behind. Caitlin, Lindsay, Sarah, Kayla, Mercy, and Nadia are just a few who held my hand on many occasions.

However, I do have to mention one person in particular whose stories, comments, and questions, made me realize what I was capable of and what I had to offer myself and the world around me. Janice was there bright and early every day with a smile, a witty remark, and a look that gave me the confidence and willpower I needed at any given moment. We would banter back and forth with each other, and she often checked in with me to make sure I was doing okay. We had nicknames for each other; I called her "J." and she called me "C." Her presence made a difference in my recovery by helping me to keep moving forward, and I cannot thank her enough.

Every staff member offered something to help me through the treatment process, and I absorbed it all. I was blessed to have these individuals touch my life. Each one gave me something that I was able to take with me and use in my recovery and they *all* have a special place in my heart.

RECOVERY TOOLS

- Letting people in
- An open mind and heart
- Honesty
- Trust
- Laughter

REFLECTIONS

Many people come and go throughout the recovery process, and each brings you something different and unique. Write the names of some people in your life who have helped you or who have been positive influences in your recovery. What have they given or taught you?

7

COMMUNICATE
WITH SUPPORTS

*"As issues came up, I was able to take each one to my peers in
the program and together we would brainstorm ways to avoid
eating disorder behaviors and incorporate new,
positive behaviors in their place."*

After a lot of hard work as an inpatient in the program, I was
considered medically stable, and it was time for me to move
on to the next phase, known as day treatment (or the partial
program). I was released to go home on the condition that I
return on a regular basis to continue my progress.

It was so nice to be back with my family in my own surroundings. I appreciated the simple things: waking up in my
own bed, sipping coffee at the kitchen table while talking to
Rachel, patting my dogs, watching the morning news. As nice
as it was, though, I knew that I needed to be aware of any triggers and continue to use healthy behaviors rather than turning
to Ed.

I showed up to the day program fully rested. It ran from
8:00 a.m. to 2:30 p.m. Monday through Friday and was on the
second floor of the same building where I had been an inpatient. The layout of the space consisted of a large group room,
a small waiting area with a sofa and chair, a dining area with a
refrigerator, a bathroom, and a few offices.

The group room was filled with chairs, bookshelves that
held games and arts and crafts, white boards, and, like the dining room, affirmations and encouragement posted all over the
walls. The only drawback was that the room didn't have any
natural light, just overhead fluorescents. For me, it was a bit

glum not to have windows, but no one else seemed to care, so I let it go. I was there for a purpose and nothing would get in my way—certainly not something as small as the lack of windows!

At home, we were responsible for following our meal plan for breakfast, dinner, and evening snack. While we were in day treatment, though, we ate a morning snack, lunch, and an afternoon snack with professional support. We ate snacks as a group in the kitchen, with usually two items to choose from. Lunch was eaten in the café where we followed our own individualized meal plans. During snacks and meals we conversed with each other and played word games as a means of support.

It was nice to be out of the inpatient hospital setting and in a more relaxed environment. There were still rules to follow, such as going to the bathroom in pairs and no talking about behaviors, calories, weight or sizes, but they were for our own safety.

In addition to supported meals, we also participated in various kinds of groups. One was based on dialectical behavior therapy (DBT), which focuses on four areas: mindfulness, interpersonal effectiveness, emotion regulation, and distress tolerance. Another group was based on cognitive-behavioral therapy (CBT), which is based on the idea that our *thoughts* cause our feelings and behaviors, not external things, like people, situations, and events. There were also groups for relapse prevention, nutrition, expressive therapy (art, dance), goal setting, yoga, and weekend planning. Each support group brought its own dynamic into my recovery plan.

One day during art therapy, Terri, the Expressive Arts Therapist, asked us to "draw a bridge to recovery." At this time, there were six of us in the group, all seated around a table in the kitchen. Unlike the group room, the kitchen had nice, natural light that came in through the windows. Music played softly in the background. There were art supplies on the table—paper, markers, crayons, pencils, and paint. We had no instructions other than to create what we imagined and felt.

I positioned myself at the end of the table near the window, grabbed the black, purple, yellow, and pink crayons and started to draw. At first, I sketched freely without thinking about it, but then the judgments crept in. I judged my drawing, my feelings about the drawing, and myself; I compared my drawing to the ones other people were doing. With each stroke, my feelings of inadequacy increased, and I became more emotional. When the negative thoughts became too overwhelming, I started to cry. I felt like such a failure. I wanted to run out of that room, to hide and be alone. I did *not* want to feel the pain or humiliation of not being good enough. I wanted it to go away!

Before entering the program, I would have "fixed" these feeling by turning to Ed or self-injury. But I could not do that any more. I *chose* not to do that any more! I forced myself to feel the experience and work through the pain and discomfort. And with the collective help of my fellow group members and Terri, I did it.

They talked me through my thoughts and feelings and allowed me to cry even as I was drawing my bridge. Terri said it was important to keep drawing as I felt these feelings, because it would give me a sense of freedom in the end. She was right. I was able to "work on" not judging myself. I could feel the release (and pain) with each line and color I put on paper. Even though the experience was a tough one, the result was positive, because I learned how to get *through* a feeling as it was happening without using a negative behavior. I felt my feelings, accepted them, and then moved on. This kind of new experience boosted my confidence tremendously.

Being in day treatment was a huge step out of the safe inpatient "cocoon" and into real life. Fortunately, as issues came up, I was able to take each one to my peers in the program and together we would brainstorm ways to avoid eating disorder behaviors and incorporate new, positive behaviors in their place. Luckily, I had the support not only from the new friendships that I made in treatment, but also from my family and friends outside the program—all of whom helped me during this most difficult part of my journey.

When day treatment came to an end, I knew I would need to test the tools I had collected there in my regular life. Learning how to handle daily work, life, and recovery stresses in a new and healthier way would be a huge challenge. But even though there would be peaks and valleys ahead, I felt ready.

RECOVERY TOOLS

- Communicating with supports
- Day treatment
- CBT
- DBT
- Support groups
- Eating with supports
- Expressive therapy (art)
- Affirmations
- Following a meal plan
- Yoga
- Crying

REFLECTIONS

Self-judgment is harsh but seems to go hand in hand with Ed. When and if you find that you're judging yourself, which of the following tools might you use to work through the negative thoughts: affirmations, journaling, chatting with supports, drawing? To see yourself in a positive, nonjudgmental light, write three positive statements about yourself.

8

MY TREATMENT TEAM

"These are complex illnesses, and I needed people who knew all about them—people who would fight Ed with me to save my life."

From the first moment I entered treatment, the faculty stressed the importance of an "outpatient treatment team," consisting of a medical doctor, a nutritionist, a psychiatrist, and a therapist. Before entering treatment, I had had a therapist and was sporadically seeing a medical doctor to check my weight, but neither of them specialized in eating disorders. They took care of me the best they could, but I needed more.

So when I was ready to leave day treatment, I knew I would have to find an outpatient team that had experience with eating disorders. These are complex illnesses, and I needed people who knew all about them—people who would fight Ed *with* me to save my life.

It was with some sadness, then, that I made the decision to find a new therapist and a new doctor. I was also on the hunt for the other two members of my team—a nutritionist and a psychiatrist. I was a bit overwhelmed by having to start from scratch, but determined to pick a team that would fit. Having the right treatment team is a vital element of recovery.

Research, referrals, questions, answers, frustration, and maintaining my patience became routine in my quest. After some time, though, it all fell into place. I am a big believer that "everything happens for a reason" and that "signs" sometimes point me in the right direction. Ever since I devoted myself to recovery, these have played out for me, and finding my treatment team was no exception.

Therapist

As I mentioned earlier, I had made a close connection with my inpatient social worker, Bob. I felt at ease with him, like I did not have to hide who I was or what I was going through, because he "got it." He saw patients with eating disorders every day! Ironically, he also worked in the same treatment facility I was in when I was first hospitalized for my eating disorder. There it was—a "sign." I knew in my heart he was the right therapist for me, so when I was in treatment and still had contact with him, I decided to go out on a limb and see if he was in private practice.

The day I decided to ask, I could hardly wait for Bob to come get me for my session. I was excited and nervous all at the same time. When he finally walked into the group room and called my name, my heart was practically beating out of my chest. Once in my room, Bob sat in a chair and I jumped on my bed, sitting cross-legged with Moo Moo clutched in my arms. On this particular day, I needed something to help with my fear and anxiety!

Throughout our conversation, my body temperature was rising, my heart continued to pound wildly, my mouth was dry, and my head started to hurt—all in anticipation of my question. Finally, Bob stood up to leave. But before he got to the door, I said, "Can I ask you a question?"

He replied, "Sure, Cheryl. What is it?"

The words came tumbling out. "Do you have a private practice, and if so, are you taking new clients?" *Oh my God, I did it, I asked him!* I sat on my bed with my eyes open wide, my body shaking and sweat building up on my forehead. I felt like I was waiting to hear if I had won the lottery!

When he said, "Yes, Cheryl, I do see patients privately and I would be happy to see you," I was elated. My insides were jumping around, I was so happy. I almost threw Moo Moo in the air in celebration. Things were starting to fall into place!

Second Therapist

A year into my recovery, I attended an eating disorder recovery workshop entitled "Divorcing Ed," which proved to be pivotal. (I will talk more about this workshop in Section Three). It was run by Thom Rutledge, a psychotherapist, author of *Embracing Fear*, and coauthor of *Life Without Ed*; Jenni Schaefer, author of *Goodbye Ed, Hello Me* and *Life Without Ed*; and facilitator Julie Merryman.

The workshop was based on Thom's intrapersonal therapy model of viewing an eating disorder (Ed) as a destructive relationship from which you need to separate, as with a divorce. Because I had read Jenni and Thom's book, I was familiar with this approach and already identifying my eating disorder as "Ed."

When I met Thom at the workshop, I found him to be honest, funny, smart, passionate, and an out-of-the-box therapist. I loved the way he worked, and was intrigued by his therapy concept. He made me think in ways I never had before and I felt lucky to have met and worked with him. Afterwards, I went to Thom's website (*www.thomrutledge.com*) to see if there was anything else there to help me in my journey. While browsing around, I immediately got excited and began to wonder if he was taking on new clients and if I could add him to my team for additional support. As usual, my mind was racing. I wanted to know right then!

I decided to email Thom and ask. I read my request over and over to be sure I had used just the right words. On pins and needles, I checked my inbox every hour to see if he had responded. *Would he write back? Would he even remember who I was? Would I have another therapist to add to my team or had my luck just run out?*

It seemed like forever, but his response came a day later I stared at it for a while, imagining what was inside. Finally I took a deep breath, double-clicked and, bingo, there it was. I swallowed hard and read Thom's message. I was thrilled. He did remember me, was taking on new clients, and was happy to make time for me! I sat there with a grin on my face from ear to ear, gratitude in my heart, and excitement running through my body. I could not believe it; I was lucky again. Another risk had paid off.

Medical Doctor

Years ago, when I was first hospitalized, I was lucky enough to work with Dr. G., a medical doctor who specialized in eating disorders. She was "the" doctor in my area for eating disorders. She was dedicated, determined, and wanted to see her patients recover. At the time, I had fallen off the recovery path and my doctor-patient relationship with her had become nonexistent. I also had heard through word of mouth that she was not taking on any new patients. I decided to call the office anyway. What did I have to lose? I knew that if it was meant to be, it would work itself out.

Again I sat on my bed with the phone in my hand and prayed that I would get something I needed. When I placed the call, I got Dr. G.'s administrative assistant. I told her who I was, why I was calling, and that I had been a patient years ago. She told me that Dr. G. was not taking on any new patients, but she would check the records to see if I was still in the system. If I was, then I was still considered a patient.

While I waited, tears filled my eyes as feelings of grief and dread bubbled up at the thought of not being able to work with Dr. G. I needed her back. I sat on the other end of the phone and hoped for another miracle.

Shortly, the assistant came back on the line, and said, "Wow, Cheryl, you're in luck." Lo and behold, my name had come up; for some reason, my information had not been deleted. Not only was I able to become an active patient again, but I wouldn't even have to wait long for an appointment, because while we were on the phone someone else had cancelled and I was able to step in.

Nutritionist

Through my research and word of mouth, I was able to find a nutritionist who also specialized in working with eating disorder patients. This was key for me, because I wanted someone who understood the inner workings of the anorexic's mind and who was willing to challenge me and show me that food is my friend. That is what I got in Amy.

I was scared to death as I went into my first session because I knew I would be talking about food, meal plans, and eating behaviors. I anticipated an anxious and emotional meeting. Even though I was extremely scared, my first meeting with Amy went very smoothly. I found her to be kind, smart, knowledgeable, respectful, and a gentle nudger. She was specific and detailed in her reasoning and explanations about why I needed to add and adjust certain foods, and she handled my anxiety with care. We talked about issues and came up with a plan that I felt I could handle. I was totally at ease and felt safe and secure talking with her about something that had previously brought me so much fear.

Psychiatrist

Because I already had a therapist, my psychiatrist's role would be to handle medication. This was a delicate subject for me, so I wanted someone who came with a reference, which is why I asked Dr. G. for a name. She gave me one and told me to tell him that I was her patient. Although his schedule was tight and he was only taking referrals, I gave Dr. M. a call and set up an appointment.

Dr. M. turned out to be caring and attentive. He listened intently when I discussed my fears and concerns about taking medication and did not ignore me or push my feelings aside. Together we came up with a plan. And with that addition, my treatment team was complete!

RECOVERY TOOLS

- Treatment team
- Asking for help
- Taking risks
- Keeping outpatient appointments
- Honesty
- Persistence

REFLECTIONS

A treatment team is vital to your recovery. Do you have one? If not, make that first call today! When searching for your team, think about what questions you will ask to be sure each professional is a good fit for you. What type of experience and/or qualities will you look for in a team? What does your ideal team look like?

9

TELL ED NO!

*"Sure, Ed kept talking away, but this time
I was talking back and telling him 'No!'"*

One morning shortly after I had begun treatment with my new team, I was in bed all cozy and warm with the dogs curled up beside me when I opened my eyes to begin my day. But before I could even speak a word or form a thought, I heard him—Ed. He was telling me what I could eat and what I couldn't, what behaviors I needed to do that day, what rules I needed to follow to make him proud, and how I needed to do it all perfectly or it would mean I had failed. According to Ed, failure was not an option.

His voice was smooth. "Cheryl, you don't need to eat breakfast today. Actually, you've been working hard at recovery, so you can take a break and skip a few meals and snacks. A few won't matter; it will be fine, trust me."

At first I thought that Ed was being my friend by watching out for me. After all, he acknowledged that I was working hard and needed a break, right? Wrong! In reality, he was being sneaky and manipulative, and nothing good would come from paying attention to him. I had to dig down deep and remind myself that everything Ed says is a lie—all of it. I needed to fight back.

So as Ed was giving me his line of crap, I decided to scream back at him and say out loud, *"No, Ed, I'm not listening to you!"* I had always been so diligent about doing what he said, but not this time. Now I wanted to leave him and live free. I wanted recovery, and I was learning to find *my* voice.

"Shut up Ed," I said. "I'm going to have breakfast, so leave me alone. Go away."

He spit back, "You don't know what you are talking about! *I* know what's best. Listen to me; you don't need to eat breakfast, you had dinner last night!"

I said, *"No Ed!* I need breakfast and I'm going to eat it. Thanks for the advice, but I'm not listening to you any more."

And with that exchange of words, I got up out of bed, went down to the kitchen, and ate my breakfast. Sure, Ed kept talking away, but this time I was talking back and telling him "No!" Although part of me wanted to listen to him and not eat, I needed to trust the process of recovery—and I knew Ed was not recovery.

RECOVERY TOOLS

- Telling Ed No!
- Following a meal plan
- Disobeying Ed

REFLECTIONS

When Ed talks to you and tells you things that are not productive for recovery, what might you say back to him? Find your voice and yell back. Write down five responses that you can say to Ed. After you write them down, say them out loud so you can hear the power behind them. Then put your voice and those words into action. Tell Ed No!

10

AN OUTPATIENT CONTRACT

"It was comforting to know I had this contract in place to keep me safe and on the right path."

My first outpatient appointment with Bob was exciting. I felt like a kid on Christmas morning, all smiles and barely able to wait to get started. But even though I was excited, Ed was not; he was talking in my ear the entire time. I told him to be quiet, that I knew what I was doing. This was a new chapter in my life—recovery—and Bob was going to be at my side all the way to guide me.

Bob's contract was a step in this process. By signing it, I had to adhere to all its (healthy) rules and guidelines. Signing a contract like that was new to me and I was unsure of what it all meant. *What if I fail at it and do not hold my end of the bargain? Will I be a disappointment?* Nonetheless, I trusted Bob, so I read what he had written and signed on the dotted line. He signed right after me and made it official. Here is the contract I signed.

TREATMENT CONTRACT FOR MAINTAINING OUTPATIENT LEVEL OF CARE

1. I must maintain medical stability as determined by my medical doctor.
2. I must be able to demonstrate weight stability and progression as determined by my outpatient nutritionist and medical doctor. A minimum of XX pound(s) per month will be expected while engaging in outpatient therapy unless weight has been restored in accordance to outpatient medical doctor and nutritionist.

3. Any "significant" weight loss or continued engagement in eating disorder behaviors that place me at medical risk or when outpatient support does not reduce the eating disorder behaviors will result in a higher level of care. This will be determined by both your outpatient treatment team and treatment facility for intensive outpatient (three to five nights of structured group program) or partial day treatment (five days per week) or inpatient treatment.
4. I must be able to ask for help or inform my outpatient therapist when feeling self-destructive, suicidal, or homicidal. I too will evaluate for any safety issues/concerns.
5. I must be compliant with scheduled outpatient appointments, follow any prescribed meal plan by nutritionist, and be open to medications recommended by my psychiatrist.
6. I will agree to have my outpatient therapist collaborate with my outpatient treatment, partner, family, and friends in an effort to support my recovery.

It was comforting to know I had this contract in place to keep me safe and on the right path. Ed was really mad about it, but in the end Bob was there to protect me—not Ed. And that is exactly what Bob did.

RECOVERY TOOLS

- Outpatient contract
- Talking back to Ed
- Talk therapy
- Trust

REFLECTIONS

A contract is put in place to keep you safe and help keep Ed away. If you don't have a contract in place, talk to your therapist about getting one. What thoughts arose for you when you were faced with a contract? What, if anything, did Ed say to you? What were your feelings after you signed it?

11

MEDICATION

"After a few weeks, it was clear to me that the medication was working. I was actually starting to hear more of my "recovery voice" instead of Ed—a taste of freedom!"

Most people with eating disorders are afraid that medication will cause them to gain weight. When Dr. P. brought up meds with me, you can bet that was the first thing on my mind. Nourishing myself and getting healthy was hard enough, but adding a treatment that could cause weight gain made it even scarier. I had many questions: *Should I take it? Will it really help me? Are there side effects? Will it make me obese?*

When the subject of meds first came up, I was terrified. I thought taking them meant I was weak because I couldn't get better on my own. Ed agreed. "Cheryl, of course you're weak. You've completely given up the rules we lived by for so long. You don't need pills, you need me." I told Ed to leave me alone and let me make up my own mind.

Dr. P. had told me that the chances of my gaining significant weight would be slim (no pun intended) to none, but my fear was deeply ingrained. So even though Ed was in my ear telling me not to, I got and read pamphlet after pamphlet on the meds Dr. P. was suggesting. I also wanted to get feedback from others who were taking them so I could "see" if what he was telling me was true. It was. The other girls on the same medications had not gained huge amounts of weight. But just hearing it from a doctor was not good enough for me at that time. I felt like I needed proof from other people who were going through it. It was hard for me to trust what he was saying, but in the end I realized he would not steer me wrong. He was there to help me recover.

So after much thought, I decided to trust the doctor and take both his advice and the medication. I hoped it would help with my racing, obsessive thoughts, because I was constantly thinking about food, food-related behaviors, and calories. I needed it to stop! I also hoped for some relief from my depression, which would help me stay motivated to stick with my recovery.

After a few weeks, it was clear that the medication was working. I was able to think more clearly and my brain didn't feel so consumed or overwhelmed. I was actually starting to hear more of my "recovery voice" instead of Ed—a taste of freedom. And in the end, my fear of weight gain was just that—a fear. Nothing drastic happened.

Today, I am still taking my meds as prescribed and following the doctor's orders. I'm also at a healthy, natural weight—another fear overcome on the road to recovery.

RECOVERY TOOLS

- An open mind and heart
- Trust
- Talking back to Ed
- Medication

REFLECTIONS

Medications help calm Ed's voice and fight depression, but the fear of taking them can get in the way. What fears or concerns do you have about taking medication? If you're already taking medication, what changes for the better have you noticed?

12

JOURNALING

"Using my journal gives a sense of respect and validation not only to my feelings, but also to whatever issue I am facing."

When I was a little girl, I got a small brown diary with a lock, and in its pages I wrote my deepest thoughts about how I was feeling and what was going on. At times my entries were about trivial things, such as who I liked in class and what my friends and I did at recess. Nonetheless, it was a place where I could express myself and get things off my mind.

As the years went by, the pages of my diary filled up and life got busy, so the writing stopped. As a result I internalized my feelings and thoughts, which worked against me because they would fester and build and eventually Ed would take over. But when my recovery started and I entered treatment, I decided to bring with me a brand new journal. It was festive-looking with lots of pages. I wasn't sure if I would ever write in it, but I knew it was there if needed.

One day when I was an inpatient, I was feeling overwhelmed and scared when my meal plan was increased and more fear foods were being introduced. I didn't want to gain more weight because I already felt like a balloon—bigger than everyone else. I wanted so badly to run to Ed for help, but realized I needed to turn to something healthy instead. So, I grabbed my journal. It took me awhile to get in the swing of it again, but as I continued to write, the feelings and thoughts flowed like a rushing river.

In the days and weeks ahead, my journal took good care of me. If I was feeling anxious because of a meal I was about to eat or a family issue I was facing, or if I was feeling sad because I felt like I was losing my best friend (Ed), or if I felt lonely, frustrated or scared, I opened my journal and put pen to paper. There, I opened my mind and heart to whatever needed to come out.

When I was writing, I never judged what I was saying or feeling, but rather gave myself permission to express anything, all the while reminding myself that "feeling the feelings" was a necessary part of recovery. Writing gave me a sense of freedom and release. My anxiety around the feelings would lessen and my mind would become clear. "Writing it out" gave me more room inside my mind, heart, and body to utilize in my recovery. I kept that journal with me and pulled it out so often that the binding was worn! I also brought it with me to my therapy sessions and frequently read from it.

To this day, I still use my journal as a tool for healthy living. It is always nearby and I can pull it out anytime to get something off my mind or get through a situation. It keeps my feelings honest and real and helps me express them in a healthy way. Using my journal gives a sense of respect and validation not only to my feelings, but also to whatever issue I am facing. It provides me a safe place to say whatever I want. Through my journal I can feel, express, accept, and work through my feelings—and then let them go. This helps me move forward in the journey of recovery and life.

RECOVERY TOOLS

- Honesty
- Self-expression
- Journaling

What healthy tool do you do to express yourself and your feelings? Do you keep everything inside and give those moments to Ed? The next time you are faced with intense feelings and thoughts, write them down and get them out of your head. Let the words flow on the page and don't judge what you write. What do you feel and how will you express it?

13

MEAL PLANNING

*"This way I didn't have anxiety each day about what I was going to have or not have, or when I would have it.
I already knew ahead of time."*

The thought of food brought me so much anxiety and fear that I was often paralyzed around choosing and preparing my meals. Somehow I needed to accept and get comfortable with seeing, touching, smelling, preparing, and tasting it. Figuring out what to eat for each meal and snack was a particularly hard struggle because Ed would always chime right in. It was a challenge to stay focused because his voice was so loud!

To help me with all that, I decided to take my meal plan requirements and create meals and snacks three days ahead of time. This way I didn't have anxiety every day about what I was going to have or not have. I already knew *ahead of time.* For three days, all I had to do was look at my list, prepare the food, and eat it. I also scheduled the times that I would eat my meals and snacks each day, so I was set with a plan that gave me a sense of safety and security. This also alleviated any fear and confusion related to food, so I could focus on more important, deeper issues.

Then, when the three days were up, I would figure out the schedule for the rest of the week and added more of my "fear foods" and foods I was craving to the meals. I knew doing this was the only way to overcome my food fears. Without a plan, I had too much time to think about what to eat or not to eat, which is when Ed would sneak in. I needed to be proactive. I didn't want him to take control, so I prepared and kept myself on track.

RECOVERY TOOLS

- Making and following a meal plan
- Taking a proactive approach

REFLECTIONS

Sit down and make a list of some of your fear foods and cravings. With your meal plan requirements at your side, take that list and plan out the next few days of meals and snacks. Don't just include your safe foods when planning; take some risks. Remember, there is no such thing as bad food. Anything goes here. Get creative and let recovery lead you.

14

SWALLOW UP

"Rather than imagine the food going 'down' into my body, I could think of it going 'up' into my brain. Eating would feed my brain, and, as a result, my mind would function properly."

One of my biggest challenges was that after each meal, my mind would go into overdrive and refuse to let go of my bad body image. With every bite that went into my mouth, I imagined the food forcing its way through my body, which was being morphed into a disfigured mess. It was mentally and emotionally painful.

One day, when I was describing the insanity of it all, my therapist Bob said, "Let's think of it in a different way." We chatted first about the reality of what happens when the brain is starved: it doesn't think straight, it becomes more delusional, thoughts become more obsessive, Ed is much louder, and there is a negative impact on concentration and affect.

Then Bob said, "Think of eating in this way, Cheryl: swallow up."

"Swallow up? What the heck are you talking about?" I asked.

He suggested that rather than imagining the food going *down* into my body, I could think of it going *up* into my brain. Eating would feed my brain, and, as a result, my mind would function properly. I thought that analogy was pretty cool, and I was ready to give it a try.

So from then on, I decided to visualize the food I ate going up instead of down. With each bite came clarity, and with clarity would come recovery. Focusing on all the benefits of nourishing my brain was a new perspective that helped get my mind out of its usual eating disorder thoughts. It was a good "reality diversion"—a diversion tactic that is rooted in reality, which gave it more power.

In thinking this way, I discovered that my recovery voice grew louder, I could focus better in therapy, my body image improved, I found laughter again, and my mind was open to more recovery and life possibilities. Thinking about swallowing up also helped take the edge off the visions I was tortured with each time I ate.

Swallowing up is a reminder of the good you are doing for yourself, not the bad. You are nourishing your brain, and when your brain is fed, you have more ability and power to fight.

RECOVERY TOOLS

- Positive thoughts
- Talk therapy
- Visualization
- Reality diversion

REFLECTIONS

Feeding your brain is essential to clear thinking. When you sit and eat a meal or snack, where do you envision your food going? What feelings do you experience? Fear, comfort, anxiety, relief? What would your "reality diversion" look like?

15

PRAYER

*"I didn't judge myself when I prayed to them;
I just opened my heart and let it happen."*

I believe in God and I believe in angels. In fact, my guardian angel has a name: Hannah. How do I know? Well, one day I sat in silence with God and the angels and asked them—and that is the name I was told. From that day forward (it has been many, many years now), I began talking to Hannah regularly. Knowing she (and God) is there for me gives me comfort. Some may not believe, but that's ok. I don't judge, and I respect everyone's own view on the subject.

So, when I began my recovery journey, without question or hesitation, I asked for God and Hannah's help. I believed that with them on my side I couldn't lose. So every day I prayed to them out loud for guidance and strength. When I did, I could feel them inside my heart and a warmth would fill my body. I could tell I was being heard. Sometimes I just talked about random things like activities of my daily life, but mostly I went to them if I felt overwhelmed, alone or fearful for the things ahead of me, which could be eating a new meal plan, confronting issues or people, expressing thoughts and feelings, or making uncomfortable healthy decisions. I would ask that they hold me up while I walked through the darkness into the unknown, and they would give me what I needed to keep going. I didn't judge myself when I prayed to them; I just opened my heart and let it happen.

At times, Ed tried to get in the way of my prayers, by casting doubt over what I was doing. "Cheryl," he would say, "no one can save you but me." That is when I prayed even harder and told Ed that he was a liar and to go away.

Prayer soothes me, helps me feel at peace, and gives me strength and comfort. Prayer helps me focus on the positive and keeps me grounded especially when Ed is determined to get me down. I use prayer daily and always will.

RECOVERY TOOLS

- Prayer
- Talking back to Ed

REFLECTIONS

Do you have a "higher power" that you look to for strength and guidance? If you don't, who or what do you look to fill that need? Do you read scriptures, pray privately (either silently, out loud, or in your journal), or pray at a place of worship? What types of things do you talk to your higher power about? Reflect on these questions and write down your most intimate beliefs.

16

THROW AWAY YOUR SCALE

"If I was going to take back control, the scale had to go. I needed to learn how my mind, body, and soul functioned together at a healthy weight and not go by a number on the scale."

"You want me to do *what?*" Had I heard right? My entire treatment team just told me to *throw away my scale?* My lifelong friend? That scale helped me stay in control, kept me on the right path, helped guide my mood! I was dependent on it. I could never throw it away. No way!

Yet every week my team kept after me, and every week I refused. This went on until it dawned on me: I trusted these people, they were looking out for me, they *wanted* me to recover. So I decided to seriously think about what they were asking of me.

After some reflection, I realized that I wasn't looking at their suggestion with a recovery mindset, because in my recovery process, I had been learning that happiness is *not the number on the scale*. Ed and the scale weren't my friends at all! They had been ruling my entire life, and I wanted to break free. Also, tossing it away meant I would truly have to trust my treatment team to know what weight was healthy for me. It seemed unimaginable—crazy even—to go through life not knowing what I weighed. The thought of never knowing "the number" scared me to death, but I was determined to conquer my fear and anxiety.

Until then, I had associated giving up the scale with giving up control. The truth was that—scale or no scale—I had never, *ever* had control; Ed did. Sure, it was my two feet that were hitting the shiny, metal surface as the number registered up at me—but from that instant on, Ed was in charge of every thought, movement, and emotion in response to that number. Cheryl had no say. Ed called all the shots, and the scale was his accomplice.

If I was going to take back control, the scale *had* to go. I needed to learn how my mind, body, and soul functioned together at a healthy weight and not go by a number on the scale. I am more than a number!

Knowing that this act of defiance would be fraught with emotion, and that I couldn't face actually physically discarding it myself, I asked Rachel to help me. We agreed on a date, which made the decision feel final. In two days, my scale would be gone for good. For the sake of accountability, I owned my decision and told my treatment team. Then it became a reality.

Finally, the day arrived. I would have to say good-bye— not later, but now. I walked into the bathroom and shut the door behind me. I felt like my best friend was moving away, like I was losing a piece of myself. My heart hurt. I moved the scale away from the wall and stepped on it one last time. As usual, it spoke back to me with that red digital number. My grief was overwhelming me, and I collapsed onto the cold floor, grabbing the scale in my arms. I held it tight to my body, cradling it like a baby, sobbing, naked, and alone. I felt as though I was losing control, even though in reality I was trying to take it back.

So there we were—Ed, my scale, and I. The Three Musketeers! How could I be so cruel as to break us up? We needed to be together, right? The pull of these emotions was very strong, but my desire for recovery was stronger. I knew if I did not leave right then, I would be in that bathroom all day. Most of all, I knew I needed to break the tie and say good-bye forever or I would never get well. After about fifteen minutes, I calmed myself down enough to stop crying, kiss the scale, and gently place it back on the floor. I was so very sad, but managed to get up and walk slowly out of the bathroom, looking back one final time.

After I left for work, Rachel got in the car and took the scale with her. As she drove down a quiet side road, she tossed it out the window where it broke into pieces, never to be seen again.

I never bought another scale. I still do not own one to this day. Don't get me wrong, I'm still tempted at times to go buy one or to weigh myself if I come across one in a store, for instance. But, when I feel that temptation, I keep my eye and mind on the bigger picture, which is recovery. The only place I get weighed today is at Dr. G.'s office, and I still step on backwards so I don't see. I take pride in not knowing how much I weigh. I do not let that number rule my mood or my life any longer.

RECOVERY TOOLS

- Throwing away your scale
- Trust
- Positive self-talk
- Crying
- Accountability

(Note: if you decide to destroy your scale, please recycle the pieces!)

REFLECTIONS

Getting rid of your scale could be an important milestone on your road to recovery. Even if you aren't quite ready yet, start the process by thinking about how you might do it. Will you smash it with a hammer or donate it? Will you do it yourself or ask a loved one to help you? Commit to a date and toss it out. You can do it!

17

A SNAP
ON THE WRIST

"When a negative thought came to mind and I began to be pulled down that road, I would 'snap' the rubber band against my wrist to shock me back into reality."

Often, during my days in recovery, I would be plagued by thoughts that would drive me towards one negative behavior after another. Ed wanted me back and he was not happy that I was committed to recovery and listening to my treatment team. I felt like there was a constant, exhausting battle going on in my head.

At times these thoughts put me into a trancelike state, caught in the middle of the battle between "Ed" and "Recovery." Ed would say, "Cheryl, I know what's best, listen to me and you will be fine, I promise." Then Recovery would say something similar, "Cheryl, listen to me, *I* am here to help you. You can trust *me*." When back-and-forth conversations like this happened, my head would tilt and my eyes would become wide and still as I just stared straight ahead, concentrating on this fight in my head.

I discovered that being in this kind of trance was a setup for disaster. In fact, the longer I was in it, the greater the chance that I would participate in a negative behavior versus a healthy one. Snapping my mind back to the here and now was extremely hard, but crucial.

So I decided to work off the word "snap" and put it to literal use. I took a rubber band and put it around my wrist like a bracelet. Having it there didn't look funny or draw attention to me in any way, so I was comfortable with it. When a negative thought came to mind and I began to be pulled down that road, I would "snap" the rubber band against my wrist to shock me back into reality. This gave me just enough of a jolt that my eyes would flicker, my head would lift up, and my mind would return to the present moment. Then I could think clearly and choose correctly—which meant choosing recovery.

RECOVERY TOOLS

- Snapping a rubber band on wrist (Note: Don't snap to induce pain or punishment, just snap to grab back your own attention.)

REFLECTIONS

During the day do you find yourself in a trance while listening to Ed and Recovery fight for you? Wear a rubber band around your wrist and snap it when you find yourself in a trance. Or list three positive steps you can take to snap you back to the reality of here and now so you can make the healthy choice.

18

ARTS AND CRAFTS

"By tuning in to my creativity, I was learning to deal with my emotions by releasing them in a healthy way."

One day, I was feeling particularly out of control because work was stressful, and I had some difficult family issues going on. Ed was screaming rule after rule at me about how I needed to do what he said to fix everything bad that was happening in my life. Deep down I knew that listening to him, and doing those negative behaviors he wanted me to do, would only bring me deeper into the trenches. But I wanted to find my way out, not get in deeper!

So to alleviate the anxiety and stress I was feeling around these life experiences and Ed's relentless bantering, I decided to arm myself with fun things to help change my mood and express myself: some coloring books, crayons, stickers, markers, paper, and glitter glue pens.

When I sat myself down at the kitchen table, the sun was shining and music was playing in the background. I was in my cozy sweatpants and slippy socks with my art supplies all around me. First I began to scribble all over a blank sheet of paper just to get out the frustration. Although Ed was telling me I was doing it wrong and the right way to express myself was to have *him* help me, I knew deep down that I shouldn't follow him (even though I wanted to). Scribbling hard with a black and red crayon seemed like a good way to release all the emotion I was feelings, so I disobeyed Ed and did that instead.

Then I moved on to my coloring book, which was Disney and had lots of my favorite characters. I picked the page with

Goofy on it because he always made me smile, and started with fun colors to help change my mood: yellow, then orange, then blue and so on.

I noticed that as I played with the various arts and crafts I had around me, my anxiety level began to decrease and my mood became more jovial. I was also singing along to the music in the background. Also, my mind was concentrating on the task at hand—not the chaos in my head. Sure, I still heard Ed screaming that I was being childish, but I pushed back and told him to be quiet and leave me alone. By tuning in to my creativity, I was learning to deal with my emotions by releasing them in a healthy way. I didn't run to Ed; I was beginning to win the war. Mmm...what next...glitter or stickers?

RECOVERY TOOLS

- Arts and crafts
- Music
- Talking back to Ed
- Disobeying Ed

REFLECTIONS

When you are stressed, filled with anxiety, or just plain mad, what might you grab to help deal with your emotions? Try going to the craft store and buying some art supplies so you have them on hand. Then, next time you find yourself filled with emotion, use that energy to create something instead. When you are done with your masterpiece, hang it up or put it in a scrapbook to remind yourself of the healthy work you accomplished. What will you make or draw? Let's find out!

19

PROS AND CONS LIST: ED VS. RECOVERY

"I had to look through the eyes of Recovery—not the camouflaged vision of Ed—to see what I was truly missing."

During one of my sessions with my therapist, Bob, he suggested that I make a list of pros and cons to compare what both Ed and Recovery had to offer. Then I could make decisions about what to do based on that information. He said he was confident that Recovery would come out on top.

So, I sat down one day with paper and pen one day and made a list with two columns: Ed versus Recovery. In one column I wrote down the things Ed offered me: loneliness, lies, isolation, bad body image, depression, manipulation, judgment, rules, a false sense of security, and other similar negatives. In the other column I wrote down the things that were the result of Recovery: freedom, strength, energy, dreams, self-acceptance, life, choices, confidence, the love of food, and other wonderful possibilities.

It was hard to get started, but after a while, the ideas just flowed. I was amazed. Recovery held many more positive things than Ed did. Even though he was a master at convincing me (and I did believe what he said) that he also had positive things to offer like comfort, safety, predictability, security, and control, I had to look through the eyes of Recovery—and not the camouflaged vision of Ed—to see what I was truly missing. This list was a powerful visual, the reality of which I could see and experience. I kept it handy, referring and adding to it often.

RECOVERY TOOLS

- Pros and cons list: Ed vs. Recovery
- Talk therapy

REFLECTIONS

To help you visualize what Ed and Recovery give to you, arm yourself with paper and pen and write out your pros and cons list. Be honest and open. You will soon see the power and possibilities that Recovery can offer.

20

PATIENCE

"We want it to happen overnight, but in reality learning entirely new ways to relate and cope takes time."

While in recovery, "Are you better yet?" was a feeling, a wish, an expectation that emanated from the people who loved me. They knew I had gone into treatment and they saw me eating, so they figured I was totally cured. However, as we know, an eating disorder is not only about the food, and recovery is not just about eating.

While I was grateful that my family and friends wanted me to be free of the pain they knew I was feeling, their hopes that I was "all better already" just added more pressure. I felt I was *expected* to make a miraculous recovery, to exhibit zero behaviors and zero anxiety, and to be in a good mood forever! It's not that quick or simple!

One day I was stressed out and anxious about an upcoming event I needed to attend. I was still learning to deal with emotions rather than react negatively to them. As Rachel and I ate dinner, she noticed that I was exhibiting some old, unhealthy rituals. She calmly brought my behavior to my attention and asked if I wanted to talk; I said no. After a few more minutes she noticed I was still having trouble and asked again. At that point, I realized I needed to reach out, so I accepted her offer and we talked about my feelings. I was frustrated that eating a meal was still difficult, but had to remember to be patient. Like Rachel was being patient with me, I had to be patient with recovery process—and myself.

Overcoming an eating disorder is a journey with twists

and turns, hills and valleys, and we must realize that we are not fixed lickety-split just because we are "in recovery" or have gone to treatment. There is no quick fix, which can be hard both for us, and our loved-ones, to accept. We want it to happen overnight, but in reality learning entirely new ways to relate and cope takes time. We must go through the process one step at a time, knowing we may take steps back before we take another step forward. All steps, no matter if they're forward or back, are still steps; we still learn.

Recovery takes time, patience, commitment, and hard work. Having the support of friends, family, and a treatment team behind you is a great foundation of strength upon which to build. Everything comes in time; be patient.

RECOVERY TOOLS

- Patience
- Talking with supports
- Eating with supports
- Following a meal plan

REFLECTIONS

Recovery takes time, hard work, and patience. Think about the last few days. Have you allowed yourself to slow down, experience, and feel each step of your process, or are you rushing through it? Take a few deep breaths and use a mantra or an affirmation for support and grounding. Example: "Recovery is a process, one that I accept with patience and love." Write down three things that you have learned over the last week about yourself or the process of *your* recovery.

21

HOLD ICE

"What I chose was a step toward recovery. I took my power back. I ran to the freezer and grabbed two ice cubes—one for each hand."

My stress level was high at the office and I was on edge. During this time, Ed was loud and I was having difficulty getting him to shut up, so I was more frustrated, anxious, and vulnerable than usual. One evening, Rachel and I got into a fight over something stupid and we ended up parting ways, one upstairs and one downstairs. I was angry and hurt, and Ed took that opening and ran with it.

He said, "Cheryl, I know what would make you feel better. Just cut yourself a little and you'll be able to make the pain go away."

And before I knew it, I was up and doing Ed's bidding. It was so fast and so automatic. There I was, starting to hurt myself when Recovery stepped in and said, *"No, don't listen to him!"* It was like someone slapped me across the face. I was jarred awake. My eyes blinked fast and I came out of the daze I was in. I immediately realized what I was doing and stopped.

Ed yelled back, "Cheryl, this **will** make you feel better. Trust me, I know you and what you need right now."

At that point, I had to really think about my next action. *What could I do to help with this anxiety and anger?* I needed to *not* listen to Ed, but at the same time I needed to listen to Recovery. Hurting myself was not going to help me through my feelings, but my mind was racing and I didn't know what to do.

What I chose was a step toward recovery. I took my power back. I ran to the freezer and grabbed two ice cubes—one for each hand. I squeezed tightly, took deep breaths, and said over and over, "Ed is wrong, Recovery is right." After a few minutes, I could feel the cold in my hands and I concentrated on that. Slowly, the voices in my head quieted down, and my anxiety and anger began to dissipate as well.

After a few minutes I dried off my hands, took a deep breath, and congratulated myself that even though I had listened to Ed in the beginning, I had intervened and changed the behavior. I faced the feelings and got through them. I did not let Ed keep the power; I took it back.

RECOVERY TOOLS

- Holding ice
- Deep breathing
- Positive mantra

REFLECTIONS

When you are faced with stressful situations or feelings and Ed is doing all the talking, do you go on autopilot? Redirect your thoughts by listening closely for the voice of Recovery; it is there. What is it saying to you? Write down three messages that Recovery can say to you when you go on autopilot.

22

SIT ON YOUR HANDS

"When I caught myself body checking, I used many techniques, which took practice. Sitting on my hands was the one I used most often, because I could do that anywhere, and it was effective."

I was told early on that recovery is not a straight line, that it has ups and downs. Until I lived it, though, I did not realize how true that statement really was. You have to fall down in order to learn how to get back up.

I fell and needed help.

Despite my progress, Ed was in my way more than I wanted him to be at this point. My food choices were becoming less risky, and I frequently skipped meals and snacks. I felt scared and vulnerable. After talking with Rachel and the rest of my outpatient treatment team, we collectively agreed that I needed a more intensive approach to move forward. So I decided to re-enter inpatient treatment, and Bob made the arrangements for me to have another intake at Walden.

Admitting I needed more help was very hard because I felt embarrassed and humiliated. My first thought was that I had failed. *How could I have let this happen?* I had to remind myself that Ed is strong and hard work is necessary to fight him off. Falling down does not mean I failed; I just needed more weapons. After I thought about it, I realized asking for help shows strength, not weakness. I hoped and prayed that Walden would accept me back into the program.

After the intake, when they came back and told me I would be staying, a sense of relief came over me. I was happy that I would get the help I sought. Another risk had paid off, and I was thankful. Even though my condition was not as medically compromised as before, the 24-hour care would help me to break the cycle of negative behaviors and thoughts. I felt some initial embarrassment about being back there again, but being around the same staff as before calmed me down right away. Comfort and a sense of security set in, and soon we were all laughing and joking together. By treating and talking to me like a person rather than an eating disorder, they helped me push through those difficult emotions.

Still, Ed was trying to convince me that I didn't have an eating disorder, and that I didn't need anyone, only him. I fought those thoughts through positive self-talk. I told myself to be brave, and remembered Bob saying I should "trust the process." I also told Ed to leave me alone.

At this point, my body checking was becoming more frequent. I was repeatedly using my hands to feel specific areas that I thought were getting bigger. I knew that wasn't good and would hinder my progress, so I told Bob. We brainstormed and came up with suggestions for ways to decrease the behavior and lower my anxiety about it.

Because I could body check anywhere and at anytime, I needed to find many different tools to help me out in various scenarios. Here's what we came up with: sitting on my hands, sitting certain ways that are comfortable, counting to fifty, journaling, putting an object in my hands, and speaking a positive mantra. I utilized any device that I could to stop the negative behavior. When I caught myself body checking, I used many of these techniques, which took practice. Sitting on my hands was the one I used most often, because I could do that anywhere, and it was effective.

Inpatient treatment provided me with new tools and experiences that made the ups and downs of my recovery begin to get easier. *But where would recovery take me next, and am I ready for it?*

RECOVERY TOOLS

- Sitting on your hands
- Asking for help
- Returning to inpatient treatment
- Talking back to Ed
- Laughter
- Positive self-talk
- Brainstorming techniques to stop body checking (such as counting to fifty, sitting comfortably, holding an object, positive mantras).

REFLECTIONS

Body checking can become excessive when Ed is constantly telling you negative things about your body. Are you listening to him? What tools can you use to stop the body checking behavior? Could you write in your journal, hold a tangible object in your hands, play with silly putty, or sit on your hands? Brainstorm with others and list 3 ways to stop the behavior. Then put them into practice the next time you find yourself body checking.

23

RESIDENTIAL TREATMENT

"Being in residential treatment helped to boost my confidence and most importantly, showed me how to incorporate food into my daily life."

As the end of my inpatient stay neared, I had to move on to the next phase of treatment, which for me would be Walden's residential program. At first I was frustrated and angry about this transition, because I wanted to go straight home. I felt like my life was on hold, but I wanted it to begin. What I did not appreciate was that learning to live without my eating disorder *was* my life. Residential treatment would continue to help me with that.

Bob walked me over to the residential facility across the street from the hospital to check the place out. On the way, my stomach was in a knot and my mind was all over the place with questions and concerns: *Will it look okay? Will I get along with the other residents? Do I really want to do this?*

The facility consisted of two apartments with four women in each. The units had two bedrooms with a private bath, a living room, eating area, and kitchen. They were comfortable, clean, and modern, complete with sofas, TVs, DVD players, and two computers with Internet access for us to use. The apartments had all the comforts of home.

There was staff on duty around the clock, and I met a few of the counselors. I also saw a couple of the other residents, but was afraid that they were staring at me, which brought up feelings of insecurity and loneliness. I felt like a puppy away from her mother for the first time. It was so different than being in the safe bubble of inpatient. *Can I do this? Am I ready? Why can't I just go home?*

This transition was difficult, but Bob assured me that "re-sie" (our nickname for residential treatment) was my next best step toward recovery. He restated his mantra: "Trust the process." I was feeling all sorts of anxiety and wanted to scream back, "Take your process and stick it!" But I sat there with my mouth shut and my mind open to what he had to say.

As I left the inpatient center with the program leader, my friends waved goodbye and wished me luck. They said, "You'll do great," and "Keep up the good work," and tears of sadness and anxiety filled my eyes. When the door shut behind me, I felt like all of my support was gone.

Although the program leader tried to be encouraging, I was appreciative yet cautious. I walked through the door with my heart in my throat, and was warmly greeted by four women, including two people I knew from inpatient, one of whom was my old roommate. That put me at ease right away and gave me a shot of courage—if they were doing it, then so could I. They helped me get comfortable with the surroundings and told me about the rules, the groups, and the goings-on; and, I started to get excited about the possibilities.

My first night was a little scary because of the unfamiliar sleeping arrangements, and my mind was spinning with all the new things to remember. However, I woke the next morning to a bright summer day. My pictures of my family stared back at me from my bureau. I went to the kitchen, grabbed a cup of coffee, sat on the sofa, and watched the morning news—just like I would do at home. I was comfortable and relaxed.

Residential treatment was all about learning to live without an eating disorder by handling life situations in a healthy way as they arose. For example, on my first day I had to face a scary (though perfectly "normal") situation—going out to lunch. Accompanied by Holly the counselor and Roberta the nutritionist, our group walked down the street to a restaurant. We were seated at a large table in a corner away from the crowd, which was good because we needed to discuss our meal plans and get advice on what and how to order.

When I looked at the menu my hands were sweating and one leg was shaking up and down. Ed was telling me to order safe, lower-calorie foods, but I had another agenda—*my recovery*. I told him to leave me alone and said, "You don't even know what I like, anyway!"

Then the waitress came to the table and said, "What can I get you?" I was barely able to get the words out, "I'll have a buffalo chicken wrap sandwich, please." It was difficult, but I stuck to my word and got what *I* wanted. I felt empowered. I had pushed through the fear and won. My sandwich even came with fries— and I ate some, too!

Throughout the meal we all chatted about our families, our work, and our struggles with Ed. We looked like just a bunch of friends out to lunch, and someone watching could not have known how hard it was for us to be eating like that in public. But we did, and survived.

Nutrition, relapse prevention, yoga, writing, and goals were just some of the groups that were incorporated throughout my days there. We went on planned outings such as shopping, pottery painting, movies, and bowling so we could incorporate fun activities into our new world of healthy living. Daily 20 minute walks, one after breakfast and one after dinner, were also included, as was working on the exercises from the web site *www.myself-help.com*.

Mealtimes happened in two shifts because the kitchen couldn't hold eight women preparing different menus all at once. We were responsible for planning, preparing, and cooking our own meals. We ordered groceries through a delivery service and could add any food we wanted to the list (except for diet food).

We were also responsible for our own messes. Chores like vacuuming, emptying the dishwasher, and putting groceries away, were split between the groups on a weekly basis. We all took turns and pitched in to take care of the place we called "home." Being in residential treatment helped to boost my confidence and most importantly, showed me how to incorporate food into my daily life. Learning to use correct portions, working with food, and preparing grocery lists and meal plans were invaluable lessons.

Visiting hours were every night after dinner for two hours. Family and friends regularly dropped by, and we could walk around the grounds with them. Unless we had a pass, we were not allowed to leave during the week. However, every weekend we had a four-hour pass and could leave the grounds if we chose. We could basically do whatever we wanted as long as we stayed within the program's rules, like not going to a gym or participating in negative behaviors.

I always went home on the weekends to see Rachel and the dogs. I loved doing simple things, like watching TV with Rachel, doing housework, and napping in my own bed. It was so relaxing and I appreciated being able to spend that intimate time with my family, especially knowing that I had worked so hard to get there.

RECOVERY TOOLS

- Residential treatment
- Having an open mind
- Talking with friends and family
- Going out to eat
- Eating fear foods
- Talking back to Ed
- Using recovery websites
- Following a meal plan
- Making grocery lists
- Taking 20-minute walks after meals

REFLECTIONS

Residential treatment has a lot of lessons to offer, including learning to respect food, gaining confidence in blending life skills and recovery, and realizing what you need and desire to continue to grow. Write down three ways you think residential treatment might benefit you and your recovery and then investigate (with support if needed) some facilities that would be a good fit for your needs.

24

A LETTER
TO YOURSELF

*"I wrote about what I accomplished, what I wanted from life,
and affirmations that spoke to me. I wrote with passion and
honesty. I didn't hold back."*

After going out to lunch on that first day in residential treatment, we were told to bring paper and a pen to our support group meeting. We were instructed to write a letter to ourselves about the positive aspects of recovery, where we were at that moment, and what we wanted. We were to put it in a self-addressed envelope and seal it up. The interesting part about this exercise was that the staff intended to mail our letters back to us six months later. I thought that was a cool twist.

I sat in the corner of the couch, staring out the window at the tree across the street and wondering what to write. I wanted to be poignant and honest. The room was quiet, and we had all strategically placed ourselves around the room for privacy.

I took a deep breath and began. I wrote about what I had accomplished so far, what I wanted from life, and affirmations that spoke to me. I wrote with passion and honesty. I didn't hold back. When I was finished, I sealed the envelope and passed it to Holly, the counselor leading this exercise.

I didn't think about that letter again until the day it arrived in my mailbox.

It was a Saturday, and I was having a particularly hard day. Holiday and work stresses dominated. Ed was annoying me, although I tried to ignore him. I flipped through the pile of mail and noticed an envelope addressed to me in my own handwriting. I was confused, but started to remember when I opened it and began to read:

Dear Self,

I am sitting in the living room of residential and it's Thursday, my first full day here. I was overwhelmed when I got here yesterday and was crying and scared. I settled in and am making myself feel at home. It was a bit challenging to make dinner and breakfast for myself, but it worked out nicely. Today we went to the restaurant for lunch and I ordered what I wanted, not what Ed wanted. It was hard to do, but I did order a buffalo chicken wrap. It was good. I ate fries, too. I had a great lunch.

I'm here at resie trying to get my life back. Learning how to fit food and feelings into my day, to be strong, and to be "normal." I want to be free of Ed's control. I want to win this battle like never before. I am building a strong foundation here with this phase of treatment and recovery. Real life is next and I want to be a part of it.

I am really learning how to live my life without the eating disorder. From the moment I open my eyes in the morning to when I shut them at night, it is a challenge to keep things real, to learn, and to feel—and most important, to eat. Despite the guilt I have for leaving my family and work again, this treatment will show me how great life is. I want to enjoy my family, my friends, my work—my life. I do not want Ed to take any of that away again. I want to rise up and be free. I just wish there was a magic pill because it is very hard to overcome, but I believe and trust my treatment team. I want to be one of their patients who has recovered. I really do love life and want to be a part of it. I want to experience all the good and bad with feelings—to feel it rather than be numb to it. I want the gift of life for myself. Stay strong and always believe!

Love,
Me
xoxoxoxo

Getting that letter was the boost I needed that day. It reminded me of what I was working toward and what I wanted to leave behind. It inspired me to be strong and confident. It arrived at exactly the right time.

RECOVERY TOOLS

- Writing a letter to yourself
- Honesty
- Residential treatment
- Support group

REFLECTIONS

Sit in a quiet place and write a positive letter to yourself. Include thoughts about where you are, where you want to go, and what you want. Seal it, stamp it, and give it to someone you trust to mail after a specified amount of time. When you receive it, you may be surprised by how much it helps. I am sure it will arrive exactly when it should.

25

CONNECT
WITH SUPPORTS

"Listening to someone who had recovered gave me confirmation that recovery is possible; plus I was able to connect with friends I'd met in treatment and make new ones, as well."

After leaving residential treatment I stayed in touch with the friends I had made there. I used those connections to aid me in my daily struggles. They knew how challenging recovery could be, and we shared many of the same goals. Having someone on the other end of the phone who understood my feelings was a tremendous help. We brainstormed and cried with each other and sometimes met for coffee or just to hang out.

On one particular day when my meal plan had just been adjusted, I remember feeling overwhelmed. Ed was telling me I didn't need to follow a new meal plan, but I knew better and called a friend. She was able to relate to my fears and frustrations and could offer me comfort. We even ate a snack together over the phone, and that helped me push Ed aside and stick to my plan.

I also utilized my family and other friends. Sometimes, when I had negative thoughts, I emailed someone or picked up the phone to get words of encouragement. Those connections kept me moving forward so that I could redirect my negative thoughts into positive ones and have a reality check. My attitude always improved when they would say, "I believe in you, I am proud of you, and you aren't alone."

Additionally, I attended a monthly support group at MEDA, my local eating disorder association (*www.medainc. org*). At each meeting a recovered person told his or her story which was followed by a question and answer session. I always seemed to find practical ideas in their stories, which I then used in my own process. Listening to someone who had recovered gave me confirmation that recovery is possible; plus I was able to connect with friends I'd met in treatment and make new ones, as well. Connections with supports are important. Laughing and crying with these people was much healthier than doing it with Ed.

RECOVERY TOOLS

- Support groups
- Socializing
- Crying
- Laughter
- Following a meal plan
- Phoning and emailing friends
- Eating with supports

REFLECTIONS

Having support is an essential piece of the recovery process. You can't do this alone. When you are having a hard time, whom can you laugh, cry, and connect with? Write down a list of people that can help you. Where might you find even more support?

26

A SEPARATION CONTRACT

"By having this written statement, I could show Ed that I meant business about wanting him gone, and at the same time show him respect for all we had been through together."

In my spare time, I volunteer for a local hospice, where I keep the patients company and run errands for them. When a person is in hospice they are treated with respect and honor as they go through the final phase of life.

I decided to relate my hospice work to my recovery by putting Ed in hospice and writing a "separation contract." I figured this would help me to say good-bye. By having this written statement, I could show Ed that I meant business about wanting him gone, and at the same time show him respect for all we had been through together.

I sat down at my kitchen table with music playing softly in the background. Feelings of extreme guilt came up as I wrote the words that would move Ed into the next phase—his death. Even though I wanted him gone, I still felt like I was doing something wrong. Nonetheless, I continued writing.

After an hour or so it was completed: Ed was transitioning into hospice, and I was the one putting him there. I was cautious but proud that I had taken another stand for myself, my life, and my recovery. Here is what I came up with:

HOSPICE REFERRAL CONTRACT

Patient Name: Ed
Patient Address: Cheryl's Body and Soul
Patient Diagnosis: Terminal Disorder

This document will serve as a referral contract for the patient named above to be admitted into Life's a Journey Hospice, a well-respected organization that offers terminally-ill patients comprehensive medical, social, nutritional, and spiritual care.

Ed will be living out the remainder of his days in familiar surroundings. Nonetheless, changing ways, an open mind, and a new outlook will be expected. The staff of Life's a Journey Hospice—Bob, Suzanne, Amy, Daniel, and Cheryl—will show Ed how to depart with dignity, comfort, and peace. They will allow him the freedom to express himself while guiding him through the new boundaries of and around death.

Respect will be shown and given by all parties, and the stages of dying will be acknowledged and dealt with as they appear. The patient will have weekly check-ins to assess his progress, and he will be given the care to see him through this difficult transition. At the end of three months, the patient will be reassessed and modifications, if needed, will be made to his plan.

The staff at Life's a Journey Hospice is committed to Ed in the quest for end-of-life care.

– Signed by me and my entire treatment team

I gave a copy to Bob and kept a copy for myself. Creating this document was both empowering and sad. But it was effective. Not only did it help prepare me to live without Ed, it also prepared Ed to live without me.

RECOVERY TOOLS

- A separation contract
- Volunteering
- Writing
- Music

REFLECTIONS

Saying good-bye to Ed is difficult, but necessary for your survival. How would your separation contract read? What would you include? Find a quiet place to write Ed's termination agreement. Authenticate it with your signature, and have your treatment team sign it. Make it official!

27

TANGIBLE OBJECTS

"On the top shelf, peering out behind a gray bunny,
was an orange giraffe. Our eyes met and I instantly knew
this was the one. A warm feeling came over me,
and I knew I had found my new friend."

As I moved away from Ed, I often felt sad and lonely over losing my best friend. Even though I had my treatment team, family, and friends, the void was heart wrenching, the grief overwhelming.

Even when these feelings enveloped me, though, I remained driven by a desire for recovery that resonated from deep inside my soul. I realized I needed to look elsewhere to fill the emptiness, and find more ways to feel loved and connected. Of course, my dogs helped me with their unconditional love, always available with wagging tails and kisses. But I had a craving for a tangible object that I could hold close to my body when I needed comfort.

I ventured out to the mall one Saturday morning with a mission: find some *thing* that spoke to me, that would make my heart warm and make me feel safe. I went from store to store, but found nothing. Ed talked to me all the while, "Why are you leaving me, Cheryl? I'm your best friend. You can't replace me. Come back to me and you won't feel alone."

But the voice of recovery countered, "Keep looking Cheryl. Ed is not your friend. You can do this." So onward I went.

In the next store, I browsed through figurines, magnets, cards, candles, and toys. When I walked into the kids' section, though, my gaze landed on a sea of plush, and I began to feel excited. Something inside of me was shifting. *I'm in the right place.* So I started sorting through the stuffed animals—dogs, cats, lambs, bunnies, and others—by picking them up and looking into their eyes. I don't know what I was looking for; I just wanted one to say, "Pick me, I'll help you."

At one point, I took a step back from the shelves to get a different view, and I saw it staring me right in the eye and calling, "I'm here, I'm here!" On the top shelf, peering out behind a gray bunny, was an orange giraffe. Our eyes met and I instantly knew this was the one. A warm feeling came over me, and I knew I had found my new friend.

After that, when I felt alone, I reached for my adorable giraffe and gave it a squeeze. It kept me company while I ate and stuck by me through difficult feelings. This little toy with the soft, cuddly body filled just enough space in my heart that I could continue to let Ed go.

RECOVERY TOOLS

- Tangible objects
- Listening to the voice of recovery

REFLECTIONS

As you leave Ed behind, finding something positive to help fill the void is a healthy step, whether it be a stuffed animal, a trinket, or a book. What items help fill your void? How do they make you feel when you hold them? Do you need to find a tangible object to give you comfort?

28

MEDITATION

"This time with myself felt like a big, warm hug—
a gift to myself and a great addition to my recovery toolbox.
Sure, Ed didn't like it, but that was the whole point!"

Many people had suggested meditation to me, but the thought of trying to sit quietly and do nothing sounded almost impossible. How could I try to just "be" when inside my head Ed was screaming the entire time? *How could that be helpful?* Nevertheless, I wanted the things that meditation could provide: more balance and energy, less anxiety, a quieter mind, and a way to replenish my soul.

So, one day, despite my skepticism, I went to a Zen meditation class. I wore comfy clothes and armed myself with my usual open mind and heart. Although my body felt tense because Ed was telling me that meditation wouldn't work, I pushed his words aside and took a spot on the floor.

The dimly lit, incense-filled room was instantly calming. The teacher instructed us to sit comfortably and close our eyes (if we felt okay doing that). Even as I heard her soft, clear voice, though, Ed was yelling in my ear, "Cheryl, you can't relax. You are being stupid and selfish!" Yet, I continued to breathe deeply and did my best to tune Ed out.

As the class progressed, I noticed that Ed seemed to get both mad and discouraged at the same time. Although he continued to shout, he could tell that I wasn't listening to him, and he backed down just enough for me to have a few moments of peace. That was all I needed to convince me to continue.

So I went back to more classes and practiced at home, surprised by how invigorating and peaceful meditation was becoming. It was dedicated quality time with myself, which gave me the space to experience tranquility, freedom, and even a sense of inner bliss. This time with myself felt like a big, warm hug—a gift to myself and a great addition to my recovery toolbox. Sure, Ed didn't like it, but that was the whole point!

RECOVERY TOOLS

- Meditation
- An open mind and heart
- Patience
- Burning incense

REFLECTIONS

How do you take quiet time for yourself? Can you sit and just "be" with your (healthy) thoughts? Give yourself permission to begin to feel what it's like to be in a quiet space—even if only for five minutes. Find a peaceful place in your house and light a candle or incense to set a relaxing mood. Listen to meditation music or instruction, and feel the shift inside of yourself. If (when) Ed speaks, push his voice from your thoughts and concentrate on your breath. Be patient and kind with yourself and don't give up. To deepen the exercise, after you meditate write in a journal about the thoughts and feelings that came up before, during, and after the meditation.

29

GOING OUT TO EAT

"I helped choose where we would go, and I banned my safe restaurants—the places Ed liked. I also stuck to my meal plan, no excuses and always incorporated fear foods."

Going out to restaurants always posed a challenge when Ed came along, because I would become extremely anxious, obsessive, and fearful. I only went to my safe places, where I knew the menu, how the meal was prepared, the calorie content, and what I would order. Ed wouldn't let me go anywhere new. But in recovery, I needed to expand my horizons to experience the joys and pleasures of trying new foods and eating in public.

So I committed to eating in restaurants—with supports—at least once a week. I helped choose where we would go, and I banned my safe restaurants—the places Ed liked. I also stuck to my meal plan, gave no excuses, and always incorporated fear foods.

I had a variety of tools to get me through those first meals. Deep breathing helped to relieve my apprehensions while I looked at the menu. I checked in with my companions while choosing what to eat. If we were seated in a booth, I positioned myself on the inside so I would feel secure with supports all around me.

I also brought along an affirmation stone with the word "Believe" on it, which I placed next to my plate for inspiration. Sometimes I actually held it for a little extra support, or I'd repeat the mantra, "I am in control, I can do this, I am okay."

To further help with my unease, I purposely focused on conversations with my friends and family members. We laughed and gossiped, but also had deep talks about personal and interesting topics. Sharing in this way not only improved my relationships, but also drowned out Ed's loud voice.

For weeks, I went out to restaurants on a regular basis, because I thought it would help lessen my anxiety and fear. But before long, I began to actually look forward to those outings!

RECOVERY TOOLS

- Eating in restaurants
- Deep breathing
- Affirmation stone
- Positive mantras
- Distracting conversation
- Socializing with friends and family
- Eating with supports
- Following a meal plan
- Eating fear foods
- Laughter
- Honesty

REFLECTIONS

What feelings are you faced with when you go out to eat? Face the fear and regain control. Make a list of restaurants you would like to try, including some that Ed doesn't like. Ask a support person (or a few) to commit to eating out with you regularly. When you go, bring some recovery tools with you. Before long, you'll enjoy eating in restaurants!

30

SELF-CARE

*"I took a moment to reflect and do some deep breathing
to become more present and appreciative. As warm water
was brushed on my face and the cleansing began, I told
myself that it was being done not just to my face, but that
Ed was being washed away, too."*

People often told me to add self-care into my recovery plan,
but I usually brushed that aside. Early on, all I could focus
on was my meal plan and the constant dialogue in my head
between me and Ed. I didn't have time for self-care. Plus Ed
said I didn't deserve it. I'd feel guilty if I did something nice
for myself!

My support team was persistent, though. So with their
help I finally decided to add something into my week that was
just for me. I booked a facial and told Ed that I was going to
pamper myself and he wasn't invited. As expected, taking time
out and spending money on me was uncomfortable and new,
but I didn't let that stop me.

At the spa, the attendants doted over me, and I enjoyed all
of the positive attention. Lying on that table, I took a moment
to reflect and do some deep breathing to become more present
and appreciative. As warm water was brushed on my face and
the cleansing began, I imagined that it was being done not just
to my face, but that Ed was being washed away, too.

To deal with my guilt afterwards, I wrote in my journal using encouraging, positive language. And when the re-
morse had subsided, my soul was singing with feelings of
power, serenity, freedom, and pride. I had done something

just for me, and it felt great.

Some of the ways I have continued to take care of myself are by having: facials, manicures, pedicures, scalp massages, full body massages, bubble baths with candles and music, quiet time in the morning with my journal, yoga sessions, and much more. I have become the Queen of Self-Care! I recognize that doing nourishing things for myself on a regular basis is healthy and empowering. The realization that I deserve to treat myself took awhile, but now I'm making up for lost time! I am worth it!

RECOVERY TOOLS

- Self-care
- Talking back to Ed
- Support
- Deep breathing
- Positive self-talk
- Journal writing

REFLECTIONS

Does Ed stop you from taking time and being nice to yourself? If he does, take a stand! Make an appointment for yourself for a facial, manicure, massage, or something similar. Before and after the appointment, write in your journal or talk with someone about your feelings, asserting that you deserve it. If you have trouble making the appointment, have a support person call for you. What self-care will you do? Enjoy!

31

RECOVERY POSTER

"Since I wanted to put my recovery poster where it would impact me the most, I found the perfect place. I hung on it my bedroom closet door, which is the first thing I see when I wake up every morning and the last thing I see when I go to bed."

Recovery was tiring work, and at times I got depressed. To help pick me up and stay focused on my goals, I decided to create a recovery poster. I hoped that looking at it would motivate me when I was feeling down.

I bought a large, pink board at a crafts store, along with markers, glitter, stickers, and glue. Then, over a period of a few weeks I gathered images and words that I found to be inspiring. Some were personal photos, others were magazine pictures that represented my hopes and dreams. I collected affirmations like, "Trust the process," "I am worth it," and "Freedom is Within Reach," as well as meaningful quotes, including one of my favorites from Eleanor Roosevelt, "You gain strength, courage and confidence by every experience in which you stop to look fear in the face. You must do the thing you think you cannot do."

Finally, I gathered up all the pieces and sat down to make my recovery poster. One by one I attached the items, happily looking over what I had selected. There were snapshots of my dogs and family members, a picture of a beautiful sunset and another of Vegas that I especially liked, because it's a place I have always dreamed of going. I added stickers of smiley faces, rainbows, dogs and stars all around and made designs with the markers, as well as numerous other embellishments.

When it was done, I felt proud of my accomplishment and I had confidence that it would make me feel empowered. Since I wanted to put my recovery poster where it would impact me the most, I found a perfect place. I hung it on my bedroom closet door, which is the first thing I see when I wake up every morning and the last thing I look at when I go to bed. It would be there to start each day with the right message and stay with me until I drifted off to sleep at night.

RECOVERY TOOLS

- Recovery poster
- Arts and crafts
- Affirmations
- Inspiring quotes and images

REFLECTIONS

What do you "look" to when you are feeling discouraged, down, or in need of motivation? Can you "see" your dreams and aspirations? Gather some images that are special to you and your recovery and make a poster of your own. Where will you put it?

32

YOGA THERAPY

"I never thought I would be able to feel positively about my body, but yoga helped me get there."

While I was in treatment, I participated in yoga classes every week to learn how to relax and connect my mind and body. I really took to it. In fact, yoga had such a positive and calming effect on me that after I left Walden I decided to add it to my recovery plan and enroll in regular classes.

As my practice of yoga deepened, I discovered many benefits. Deep breathing and quieting my mind allowed me to disconnect from negative thoughts. Controlling my breath during the poses provided a calmness and serenity that carried over into my life, because when I felt calm, my mind was open to new, healthy possibilities. With the daily practice of yoga and the breath, my soul felt centered, nourished, and refreshed.

Yoga also helped me to experience a strength inside my physical body that I never knew existed before. As a result, I began to feel, appreciate, and respect what I once despised. I never thought I would be able to feel positively about my body, but yoga helped me get there.

Yoga soon became a favorite recovery tool. Depending on the situation I was facing, I did deep breathing, a yoga posture, or a meditation, any of which helped me through difficult moments of anxiety, stress, doubt, or fear. Centering myself when I was having a tough time connected me to an inner wisdom and strength from which I could gain a healthy perspective.

Yoga is a great way to calm down, improve your relationship with your body, and take a break from the hectic rituals of everyday life. It draws you into a quiet place where just you and the Universe exist. Your mind, body, heart, and soul become one.

RECOVERY TOOLS

- Yoga
- Deep breathing
- Meditation

REFLECTIONS

Yoga is a calming practice that helps relieve anxiety and fear. When you are faced with difficult situations and Ed is talking to you, what can you do to calm yourself down? Listen to music, do yoga, breathe deeply? Write down five ways to calm yourself, find stability, and be in the present moment.

33

HONESTY

"Being honest with myself and allowing myself to get the help I needed, demonstrated my strength, determination, and will to get better, and it proved who was really in charge of my life—ME!"

As the holidays approached, life became hectic, and I was stressed out at work. Ed was talking to me more often, begging me to play his games. Since I was around food at holiday parties, he was moving in on my weaknesses and vulnerabilities. Sometimes I listened, but other times defied him, which showed me that I still had the will to fight him off.

The day after Christmas, Rachel and I went to see an exhibit at the Museum of Science. We had one stop to make first—my session with Bob. I was eager to talk about my recent trouble with Ed because I knew it was a red flag. I wanted to be honest, but I was nervous. It didn't help that Ed was telling me everything was fine.

At my session I came right out and told Bob, "Ed is getting in my way, and I am scared because my meal plan, my mood, and my thoughts are being influenced. I'm afraid that Ed won't let go and that I'll follow him wherever he wants to lead me." As soon as I spoke those words, I felt a sense of relief and pride because I knew I was being honest with myself, and with Bob, about where I was with Ed.

So Bob said, "Let's figure out a plan." We chatted about the variety of tactics I was using to fight Ed as well as what new tools I could use to put him in his place. Then at the end of the session, he asked, "What do you think about going back to treatment for a short while—for a bit of a boost?"

To my own surprise, I answered, "Can I think about it?" And I left promising I would call later with my answer.

As Rachel and I continued with our plans at the museum, I pondered what might lie ahead—leaving my family again, more treatment, and the thought of people knowing about it. After seeing the exhibit, we grabbed a bite to eat and chatted about the possibility. I began to feel guilty at the thought of doing something for myself again. *How I could be so selfish?* I also began to feel afraid because I knew Ed was close by. When I shared my feelings with Rachel, she said without hesitation, "You should go, Cheryl; it will only make you stronger." That was the confirmation I needed to return to treatment.

Having made a decision, I excused myself from our meal and told Rachel I'd be right back. I took my phone outside into the cold air. People were walking in and out of the mall, milling about and doing their thing—and I was doing mine. With confidence and no fear or hesitation, I dialed Bob's number and said, "I'm taking you up on your offer."

He replied "Great, I'll make the arrangements and they will call you tomorrow." And with that, I went home and packed.

Although I had 10 days between Christmas and New Year's Day off from work, being in treatment was not how I wanted to spend my time. But in my heart I knew I needed it to continue showing Ed that I wanted him gone forever. Being honest with myself and allowing myself to get the help I needed, demonstrated my strength, determination, and will to get better, and it proved who was really in charge of my life—ME!

Bob called the next morning and said, "Be here at 1:00 PM."

I replied, "Will do, thanks." And with that I was on my way to Walden for a tune-up.

Walking in felt different this time because I was not embarrassed to be there. I held my head high and acknowledged all the hard work I had done to get to this point. I was much farther along in recovery, and happy for this opportunity to get back on track.

During this stay, I reflected on the past year and what I had learned about myself, Ed, and life. I shared my insights during groups and with new friends, discussing steps that worked and those that didn't, and exchanging new ideas. I rang in the New Year while in treatment, and chose to view it as a motivator rather than something negative. And my unforgettable experiences during those days gave me the boost I needed to continue my journey towards full and lasting recovery.

RECOVERY TOOLS

- Honesty
- Keeping outpatient appointments
- Talk therapy
- Inpatient treatment
- Reflection
- Eating with supports
- Talking back to Ed
- Communicating with supports
- Being open

REFLECTIONS

Are you being honest with yourself about your struggles with Ed? Reflect on what is happening for you right now. Are you in need of a tune-up? If so, remember that returning to treatment does not equal failure; it equals strength. What could you do to give yourself that boost to keep going? In other words, what would a tune-up look like for you?

34

FEELINGS BOX

"Combining deep breathing with the physical act of 'tearing through' my pent-up feelings, or crumpling the paper, added to the release."

When I was struggling with Ed, I was often numb to my emotions. But as I moved forward in recovery, I learned the importance of experiencing all my feelings—the good, the bad, and the ugly—and dealing with them appropriately rather than running to Ed.

Many times I would find myself filled with a jumble of conflicting emotions not knowing what to do with them. And then I discovered that writing down the names of the emotions lessened their power. Whether it was anger, frustration, or disgust, I would write those words down on paper and feel better. Sometimes I would write a letter to Ed expressing how I hated him. Other times I just wrote random words or scribbles that conveyed how I felt. Most important, I was getting these feelings out of my system by accepting and expressing them in a safe way.

Taking that one step further, I came up with another way to release my emotions so they wouldn't harm me, or my progress. One Saturday I went to my local craft store and purchased a small, wooden box along with paint, glitter, stickers, and stencils. Returning home with my goodies, I put some music on and decorated the box. The finished product had a bright, cheerful look, which was important to me because it was going to hold my deepest, most intense feelings.

After I had written my feelings down—whether in the

form of a letter, a word, or a doodle—I tore the paper into small pieces or crumpled it up in my hands while exhaling slowly. Combining deep breathing with the physical act of "tearing through" my pent-up feelings, or crumpling the paper, added to the release. I then placed the pieces in the box, closed the cover, said, "See ya," and walked away. By acknowledging, feeling, accepting and releasing these emotions, I knew the negativity could no longer hold me back, and I would feel free.

RECOVERY TOOLS

- Feelings box
- Writing
- Arts and crafts
- Music

REFLECTIONS

Do you have a healthy way to rid your body of pent-up emotion that could be holding back your recovery? Try making a Feelings Box. Find a place for it to live and visit it each time you have a negative emotion you want to let go. Feel, accept, and express the emotion as you place it in the box to say good-bye. After you walk away, check in with yourself and write down five words that describe how you are now feeling.

35

MASSAGE

"When I leave that tranquil space, I am ready to face the world with a sense of wholeness, because I know that my mind and body are learning to become friends."

Lying naked on a table while someone rubs you down is a luxury for most people. For me, though, it's therapy, because being in tune with and connected to my body is important for my recovery. So I go to my massage therapist, Erin, every other week. And because she knows my history with Ed and my problems with body image, she is especially sensitive to my fears and feelings.

One would think it would be excruciating for a person with an eating disorder to have someone touch the very thing they despise, but for me massage is actually healing. It brings up feelings of strength, power, acceptance, and a sense of freedom from my poor body image and negative thoughts. Getting to that point took time and courage, but when I was ready to take the risk and push through the fear of exposing myself—emotionally and physically—the rewards were definitely worth it.

I remove my clothes, lie down on the table under the covers, take a deep breath, and for the 90 minutes I am on that table, my mind and body become one. Sure, for the first thirty seconds Ed tries to jump in and tell me that I am so big that my fat is hanging over the table, but I talk back and tell him he is a jerk. I want to learn to live in my body and accept it, no matter what its size. So, I reframe the negative thoughts into positive ones, and before I know it my mind is in tune with what Erin is doing.

When I am on the table, I actually experience my body from the inside out. I feel light all over, and I can sense the energy inside. I do not judge myself. Massage therapy helps me become more mindful of my physical self, and am aware of my body as the instrument and gift that it is— instead of thinking it's my enemy. When I leave that tranquil space, I am ready to face the world with a sense of wholeness, because I know that my mind and body are learning to become friends.

RECOVERY TOOLS

- Massage
- Talking back to Ed
- Deep breathing
- Reframing

REFLECTIONS

Making peace with your body is a challenge for anyone, but particularly for someone in recovery from an eating disorder. But you *can* accomplish it. Think about your body. Are you connecting with it or ignoring it? Write down three ways you could have a more positive relationship with your body.

36

USE YOUR SENSES

"Scents also give me the feeling of being hugged and that comfort gives me a sense of power and strength, like I can accomplish anything."

Some days Ed is in my head and won't let go. I try to shake him off, but he hangs on tight. He tells me I need to listen to him to get through my day, and if I don't, my body will expand like a balloon and nobody will want to look at me.

Usually, I use tools like positive self-talk and talking back to Ed, but sometimes I need a distraction to give my mind a jolt. This jolt then gives me just enough of an edge to turn my thinking towards something positive and healthy. For this purpose, I use my senses of touch and smell.

Touching something that is textured gives my mind an alternative place to go. The feeling in my hand goes through my body, and before I know it, my mind is concentrating on the touch and feel of the object. I use a variety of items: a pillow with soft fringe, a squishy, gel-filled ball with spines on it, a smooth marble heart, and an affirmation stone. If I am feeling anxious, I might go for the soft feel of the pillow or the smooth stone. If I am feeling angry, I will grab the gel ball and squeeze the heck out of it.

I also use my sense of smell. When I feel anxious, frustrated, or angry, aromas turn my awareness inward, which is centering and soothing. Scents also give me the feeling of being hugged and that comfort gives me a sense of power and strength, like I can accomplish anything. I keep various scented objects—candles, incense, air fresheners from my car, scented oils, flowers—close by so they are right there when I need them. Some of the scents that help me are lavender, clean cotton, the smell of fresh laundry, strawberry, wood, baking bread or cookies, and my favorite—coffee.

All of these things give me just enough of a distraction to keep Ed at bay and let the voice of Recovery chime in and take over.

RECOVERY TOOLS

- Touching something textured
- Scents

REFLECTIONS

Your senses are always available and can be quickly utilized for your benefit. Do you have a favorite smell or texture that might help give your mind a jolt when Ed is in the way? Look around the house and grab a few things. Touch them; smell them. How do they make you feel? Choose a few that make you feel happy, safe, and secure or that command your attention, and keep them handy for when you need them.

37

SUPPORT LIST

"I needed to overcome the fear of asking for help, as well as understand that asking meant I was strong and not weak."

Inevitably, there were some days when stress would strike, Ed's voice would be loud, and my recovery voice would be difficult to hear. I would find my thoughts spinning in a hundred directions and wouldn't know which one to move towards. During these times, I needed to reach out to other people to help ground me in the present moment. I knew this would be a challenge, but I also knew I couldn't get better alone—my treatment team had taught me that. What's more, I needed to overcome the fear of asking for help, as well as understand that asking meant I was strong and not weak.

So, I sat down one day and made out a list of all the people that I thought would make good supports. Next to their name I listed their contact information as well as what kind of support they would best be able to offer. As I was sitting there, Ed chimed in and told me that no one could help me like he did. He said, "I know you better than you know yourself, Cheryl! Don't be foolish and think you can go to others. Stick with me." Even though I wanted to agree with him, I told him that I have "real" support people I can trust, and he is not one of them.

I continued to make my list in spite of Ed's pleas. I chose my supports carefully, keeping in mind that not everyone understands how completely Ed can take over the mind and the "craziness" that goes along with that. Also, support people are only capable of giving what they can, which might not be all I might need at the time I reach out. This is why having a variety of people with different skill sets on your list is important. Some people make good listeners, or might be good at brainstorming, while others may be great eating companions, or serve as an effective distraction. Some friends will enjoy food shopping and others will be good problem solvers. Each person will have his or her own strength from which to draw.

Once my list of supports was complete I put one copy in my purse and another by the phone and computer. Having it readily accessible in different places made it easier to know whom to call or email when I was in the middle of a panic and couldn't think straight. A little preparedness can help during high stress moments, and having a good support list is a great start!

RECOVERY TOOLS

- Support List
- Talking back to Ed

REFLECTIONS

Make a list of the people you have in your life who might make good supports (maybe using crayon or marker to make it more colorful and fun). Be sure to include their contact information. Are they family members, friends, professionals, church members, or co-workers? How has each one helped you in the past? Then list each person's strengths. Get as creative as you consider how these strengths might dovetail with your particular wants or needs. Put a copy wherever you can get to it quickly—in your purse or book bag, on your phone or computer. This way, when you are in need of additional support, you can reach out right away and get help. Who will you contact when you are in need?

38

CONVERSATION TOPICS

"I knew I couldn't control what others would say in any given situation, but I could control my reaction. "

Usually, attending parties, dinners and other social events caused me anxiety about things like the food, what I would wear, who would be there, who wouldn't be there, and what people would be talking about. I was especially worried about triggering comments on subjects related to appearance and dieting. In most situations where I felt uncomfortable and it was feasible to do so, I would remove myself by walking away. But when I couldn't, I needed a plan to protect myself and my recovery.

I decided to make a list of safe conversation topics that I could put in my Blackberry "notes" so it wouldn't be obvious when I referred to it. This list would be comprised of a variety of topics such as my upcoming vacation, a project at work, my dogs, my niece and nephews activities, the latest celebrity issues, a recent news clip, or the latest technology gadget. When I was faced with conversation that didn't feel right, I used my list of topics to change the subject, help guide the conversation, or fill in the silence.

Having this list helped me feel safe so I wasn't scared or triggered. I knew I couldn't control what others would say in any given situation, but I could control my reaction. Having a plan to help me through difficult conversation situations relieved stress, gave me confidence, and was also interesting and fun! What can I talk about next?

RECOVERY TOOLS

- Having conversation topics

REFLECTIONS

To help you keep the conversation flowing in a positive, fun note, what would you talk about? Before you go to a party or out with family or friends, make a list of things that you could bring up to spark conversation, like what you did that day, your pets, or a class that you just took? Make a short list and put it in your phone/Blackberry so you can refer to it easily and comfortably. What's on your list?

39

ONE BY ONE

*"Every fourth day I would review what I had already learned—
to keep it fresh and alive—and then started to work on
the next Ed-based behavior. I was always pushing
myself to grow. This was moving me forward!"*

When it became clear to me that I would need to stop all Ed-based behaviors and replace them with healthy recovery-based ones, I felt overwhelmed. My habits were mine! They had helped guide me and keep me safe, right? No! None of my negative behaviors were improving my life, but I knew it would be difficult to stop them all at once. Talk about stress, pressure, anxiety, and fear!

With this in mind, I began to pay more attention to what I was doing every day, and I discovered that sometimes I wasn't sure if a particular behavior was Ed-based or recovery-based. This made it hard to decide if I should stop it or not. To help me sort this out, I did two things. First, I made sure I was hyper vigilant about what I was doing and if a certain pattern came up, I would write it down so I wouldn't forget it. Then, when I was done, I brought the list to Bob and we determined what was Ed- based and what wasn't.

With Bob's help, I was able to visit each behavior and soon began to realize that most of them were primarily Ed-based, with instructions from him on what to do, how to do it, and why. They were also based on avoidance of feelings and coping in unhealthy ways. While writing down these negative patterns and being honest about them helped me open up and gave me goals to achieve, giving them *all* up seemed like an overwhelming job. I was afraid and sad, yet determined to succeed.

To help deal with my anxiety and fear I came up with a plan: I would work on one behavior every three days. During those three days I would pay extra attention to what I was doing, and when one particular destructive behavior came up, I would use a variety of recovery tools to stop it. For instance, I could write in my journal, listen to music, cry, or reach out to a friend. Every time I swapped the Ed-based habit with one that was recovery-based, I felt a tremendous sense of accomplishment and pride. Then, every fourth day I would review what I had already learned—to keep it fresh and alive—and then started to work on the next Ed-based behavior. I was always pushing myself to grow. This was moving me forward!

When I put this plan into place, Ed was quite vocal. He insisted that my old habits were keeping me safe and in control, and I needed them. He would also try to convince me that I didn't need to work so hard, that I could take a break between goals and go back to them at another time. So I had to remain strong and continue to work on *all* behaviors no matter what Ed said—even if he sounded like he was trying to take care of me. I had to remember that Ed lies. He only cares about himself and his plan, not mine. And he has no place in my recovery.

Ending negative behavior patterns is key to recovery and doing so was not easy, nor did it happen all at once! But being aware and honest about them, and committing to systematically transforming them, one by one, into a positive, recovery-based life gave me a compass to guide me along my road to recovery.

RECOVERY TOOLS

- Taking steps one by one
- Journaling
- Crying
- Supports
- Music

Have you been able to look at your Ed-based behaviors head-on? Have you been honest about what they are? Begin to take charge by making a list of patterns you recognize. Also brainstorm with your treatment team or a loved one about any they notice. After the list is complete, commit to working on one behavior at a time for three days. When you move on to the next one, don't forget to continue your successful work on the ones you have already faced! Over time, you will replace the Ed behaviors with healthy ones and freedom will be around the corner. You are strong. You can do this. What behavior will you stop first?

SECTION 3

BREAKING THE CHAINS— SEPARATION AND STRENGTH

40

ROLE-PLAYING: SEEING THE SEPARATION

"I knew right then that I was not Ed and Ed was not me. I was my own person. And now I had something and someone to fight, instead of fighting against myself."

As I mentioned previously, I read the book *Life Without Ed* and was intrigued by the therapeutic approach of the co-author, Thom Rutledge. Browsing his website (*www.thomrutledge. com*) one day, I found that he was offering a "Divorcing Ed" workshop with his co-author Jenni Schaefer, and another facilitator, Julie (Jules) Merryman. The workshop really interested me, but it was being held in Tennessee, far from my home in Massachusetts. Did I want to spend the money and take the risk? Besides, Ed was telling me I was fine and that I didn't want or need what they were offering. He was also telling me that I did not deserve to go.

Nevertheless, after heated debate with Ed and lots of email support from Jules, I decided to take the plunge. I sent in the fee, booked the hotel, and jumped on a plane not knowing what was in store. It felt surreal, but somehow right. A thousand questions ran through my mind. *Would I find what I was looking for? Would I meet new friends? Could I do this while Ed was screaming at me every step of the way?* I knew I was in for a tough weekend and hoped I was prepared.

Even though I was used to referring to my eating disorder as Ed, I still was not able to fully separate myself from him. After all, he had been with me my entire life, and I did not fully know who Cheryl was without him. I was still a prisoner, intertwined in ways I didn't fully understand. I hoped this workshop would help me see and feel the separation between the two, even for a short time. I never expected to get what I got!

I arrived at the workshop with 19 other women from all walks of life. We may have been different in many ways, but we had Ed in common and could relate to each other in ways many other people couldn't.

I remember walking into the room on that hot, sunny Saturday with new friends and a spring in my step, ready to do any work that would help me grow. Thom, Jenni, and Jules had set it up with all the comforts of home: big pillows on the floor, blankets, music, low lighting, and snacks and beverages. It felt safe and warm right from the start.

When the workshop began, Thom said, "Let's start with some role-playing." *Role-playing, what the heck is that?* I didn't understand at first because this technique was new to me, but it soon became clear. We formed a circle around Jenni and Thom, with Jenni playing herself, and Thom playing the role of Ed.

When they began, the scenario and the words being spoken were all too familiar. Ed was being so persistent, so degrading, so bossy, and so manipulative that it hit home— hard. He was trying to control Jenni, but she was fighting back. "I don't need you Ed, leave me alone!"

Then Ed tried to woo her back by saying, "You need me, Jenni. We are friends and I won't disappoint you, I'm here for you."

But Jenni was strong and stood her ground saying, "*No,* I'm not listening to you anymore, Ed!"

As I sat there staring at the two of them with my eyes open wide and my mouth hanging open, I couldn't believe what I was seeing and hearing! It was all becoming so clear: the words, the threats, the responses, the fights all played out—live—right in front of me! The realization I was having was overpowering. It felt like someone came running toward me, grabbed me by the shoulders, and shook me hard while looking into my eyes and screaming, "Wake up! Do you see it now?" Indeed, at that moment, through Thom's exercise, I finally *did* see that I am *not* my eating disorder. Ed *is separate* from me. I was stunned, in disbelief. It took me a minute to compose myself. *Did I just see what I think I saw? Is this real?*

Witnessing the battle that I fought every minute of my existence gave me a sense of identity I had never had before. I knew right then that I was not Ed and Ed was not me. I was my own person. And now I had something and someone to fight, instead of fighting against myself. From that moment on, I had new hope and strength, which I decided to use to my advantage in my fight for myself. Trust me when I tell you that you are *not* your eating disorder!

RECOVERY TOOLS

- Role-playing
- Talking back to Ed
- Taking risks
- An open mind and heart
- Recovery workshops
- Trust
- Intrapersonal therapy

REFLECTIONS

Knowing and believing that you and Ed are separate is a key in your fight for freedom. Working directly with Thom's exercise, ask a member of your treatment team or a strong support to role-play with you. Take turns being Ed. As you converse with each other, listen carefully to the dialogue. As you practice, it will become easier to distinguish between your voice and Ed's. You will realize that the two of you are separate; you are not the same. (If role-playing is difficult or can't be done, then write down a conversation between you and Ed to get the same effect).

41

THE FIVE
MESSAGES EXERCISE

*"I left that weekend with a sense of hope and strength
that I had never experienced before. I had heard and felt
Recovery—I knew it could be done."*

I didn't expect to get another "Aha!" moment from Thom's workshop, but the "Five Messages" exercise provided just that. Our instructions were to write down five statements Ed often makes, adding our name in front of each one. Here are mine:

1. Cheryl, you will only be successful and liked if you stay loyal to me.
2. Cheryl, you can't eat that because it will make you fatter.
3. Cheryl, I am the only one who matters in your life; everyone else doesn't.
4. Cheryl, you are fat and ugly.
5. Cheryl, you and I are connected as one because we've been together for over 22 years, and that commitment to each other should not be broken. You'd better not leave me, because I wouldn't leave you.

After we wrote our messages, we broke into groups so we could listen to other people read them. We could also position support people around us and tell Ed where to sit. I put him in front of me slightly to the left, since that is where he had been my entire life. When it was my turn, Jenni, who was overseeing our group, asked if she could do something that had worked for her. Indicating I was open to it, she moved closer and sat back-to-back with me.

So, while Ed's remarks were being read aloud, I had support people all around me, which was tremendously empowering. I felt both strong enough to hear Ed's words, and unwilling to retreat in fear. Actually, I couldn't, because Jenni was supporting me from behind! Although I was right in Ed's path, I was not alone.

After we finished this part of the exercise, I experienced lots of feelings: anger at Ed for treating me so poorly and telling me such horrible things (even though it was hard not to believe him), powerful with my supports around me, and determined that I would change my reactions to his lies and manipulation. Hearing Ed's messages to others also helped me recognize that he indeed was cruel, did lie, and didn't love me—or anyone. If he did, why would he say such horrible and threatening things?

Later in the day, we continued the exercise by writing down five "recovery messages" (even if we did not believe them at the time). Here are mine:

1. Cheryl, being in recovery shows strength.
2. Cheryl, you are well liked and loved.
3. Cheryl, trust your treatment team.
4. Cheryl, it does get better.
5. Cheryl, a friendship with food is a positive thing.

We then broke up into groups and read our statements out loud. When we were finished with each one, the group would affirm, "Cheryl, this is true."

Again, we chose where our Recovery "voice" and our supports would be positioned. I had my Recovery voice in front and slightly to the right, because that is the direction from which I always hear it. I asked that Jenni be a recovery support as well, because she was behind me during the first exercise and I wanted to come full circle. With Jenni at my back, it was possible for me to reach behind and hold her hands. The others gathered around.

As the exercise began and my positive messages were slowly read aloud, I could hear the voice of Recovery coming at me with gentle force. The part where the group said, "Cheryl, this is true" really hit home. I could sense the vibrations of Jenni's voice through her hands. Her strength, hope, and truth moved through my body and touched deep inside my heart and soul. My body felt like it had been struck by lighting—numb yet alive all in the same moment. I was literally "feeling recovery" through the energy of someone who's been there. I was being given the power and hope I needed—a gift beyond measure.

When the exercise was over, we left our groups and mingled. The day was coming to a close, but before I knew what was happening, my entire body began to shake, my eyes filled with tears, and my heart was overcome with emotion. I was vulnerable. In a matter of moments, it all came out and I broke down sobbing right there in front of everyone. I felt like my body was filled with light pulsing throughout my entire system. Everyone came to my aid and held me tight. All I could say was "I can do this, I really can do this. Thank you."

I left that weekend with a sense of hope and strength that I had never experienced before. I had heard and felt Recovery—and I knew it could be done. Being a part of Thom's workshop, and making new, intimate friendships there, had done more for me than I expected or even imagined. It was my turning point.

RECOVERY TOOLS

- Five Messages exercise
- Support people
- Honesty
- An open mind and heart
- Acceptance
- Crying
- Recovery workshops

REFLECTIONS

Try Thom's exercise. Find a quiet place and write down five statements that Ed says to you and then five statements Recovery says to you (even if you don't believe them yet). Gather a few supports or take them to your support group or therapist and have them read back to you. Listen closely, take it all in, and experience it. Feel the power and hope of recovery around you. Feel your strength. Know that you *can* recover.

42

RECOVERY
REMINDERS

*"Within half an hour, I had a reminder of recovery on my body
forever. I could not have been happier. I walked away feeling
powerful and protected. From that point forward, all I had to
do was look down, and see it shining right up at me."*

While at Thom's workshop, I found out about the "Life Without Ed" Collection, which was created by Sue Gillerlain, jewelry designer and founder of *www.sarah-kate.com*, in partnership
with Jenni Schaefer, author of the book by the same name. I
was lucky enough to be able to purchase a necklace with a
flower on it—a symbol of strength for me. It hangs close to
my heart.

Because of the power and significance this flower pos-
sesses for me, I wanted to make it a permanent fixture in my
life—one I could look at whenever I needed a tool to help me.
So, I decided to have the flower tattooed on my body. This
symbol of the experiences of recovery I had at Thom's workshop would always be there for me to see, remember, and feel.

I knew exactly where to put it: on the inside of my left
ankle. In the past I had practiced self-injurious behaviors on
that area of my body, and I wanted my flower to be a reminder
to always take care of myself, rather than hurt myself.

I got the name of a tattoo artist from a friend and called
him up. He said he was going to be at a tattoo convention in a
town about an hour away the following weekend. Good sign! I
told him what I wanted, and he said it wouldn't be a problem
at all. I should come by and see him.

That Saturday I woke with excitement bubbling in my belly.

The convention didn't start until late afternoon, and the day seemed endless! By the time Rachel and I finally walked into the hall, I was fidgeting with joy and anticipation, my hands were tingling, and my stomach was doing flips. Eventually we made our way to the artist's table and I introduced myself. He said, "Glad you're here, Cheryl, have a seat. What have you got for me?"

I took my necklace from around my neck and explained, "I want this flower on the inside of my left ankle."

He took the charm and did his magic. Within five minutes he had traced the flower on my ankle and asked, "How's this?"

"Perfect," I said. "Let's do it." And away he went.

As he was working, I was smiling from ear to ear, proud of myself for having the courage to get where I was. I was winning the fight. Within half an hour, I had a reminder of recovery on my body forever. I could not have been happier. I walked away feeling powerful and protected. From that point forward, all I had to do was look down, and see it shining right up at me.

RECOVERY TOOLS

- Recovery reminders

REFLECTIONS

Recovery reminders come in many forms: jewelry, posters, seashells, stones or gems, letters, tattoos—whatever holds significance for you. What might you use to give you strength when you need it?

43

TALKING TO ED

"I didn't realize that Ed actually sounded different than me, or that he had a separate persona! How would I? Ed had never spoken out loud to anyone else before—only to me."

As I mentioned in Chapter 8, I contacted therapist and author Thom Rutledge after his workshop to see if he would do phone consultations with me, and he gladly agreed. Our first session took place on a 90-degree day in July. As I dialed the number, my belly was doing its usual flips. *How is this going to go? Will I get anything out of it?* Then the phone began to ring, and I heard, "Hello, this is Thom."

My voice quivered a bit as I said, "Hi, Thom. It's Cheryl Kerrigan." And the conversation began.

We were chatting about the work I had done at the workshop and my recovery steps thus far when he asked me something that threw me for a loop.

"Would you be willing to role-play? I want to talk to Ed."

"I've never done that before" I answered. "I don't know if I will do it right."

He reassured me. "If you are open to it, it will just happen. Ed will be there."

With fear in my voice I agreed.

My heart was beating out of my chest when Thom asked the first question, "Ed, what are your intentions for Cheryl?"

"To make her happy, of course," Ed replied.

"How do you make her happy, and what is your relationship?" Thom asked.

"I've been with Cheryl for a long time, Thom. I know what she needs and wants—you don't!"

"Ed, how do you know what's best for her?"

"I just do."

"That's not an answer. I want specifics," Thom pressed.

"You are so stupid, Thom. You don't know what you are talking about. She needs me."

"No she doesn't, Ed. You are wrong."

Right from the start Ed was on the defensive, but Thom was persistent and gave it right back without backing down. When Thom asked Ed for specifics or to explain himself, he lashed out with insults and lame answers. He did not like to be questioned. He tried to show Thom that he was in charge, but Thom would not give him that position of power. This went on for about fifteen minutes.

Afterwards, Thom gave me feedback, which blew my mind. He told me that when Ed speaks, his voice is low and monotone. He also said that Ed came across as an overconfident jerk. I was shocked. I didn't realize that Ed actually sounded different than me, or that he had a separate persona! How would I? Ed had never spoken out loud to anyone else before—only to me.

Then Thom asked me to listen carefully to Ed's answer to the next question, concentrating on the sound of his voice.

"Ed, what have you done for Cheryl today?"

"I do *everything* for Cheryl, Thom. Leave us alone. You don't know anything."

When I heard that answer, I couldn't believe my ears. "Oh my God, Thom, I can *hear* him, I can really *hear* him!" Ed's voice really *was* different than mine and he *was* acting like an overconfident jerk. I could feel it and hear it for the first time ever. I was totally freaking out. I was amazed!

So my first conversation with Thom was incredible. With an open mind and heart, I had gone out on a limb, role-played for the first time, and truly learned from it. I couldn't wait until we would talk again.

RECOVERY TOOLS

- Talking to Ed (role-play)
- An open mind and heart

REFLECTIONS

When you're living with Ed, you might be listening to what he says, but not think of him as a separate person. The next time Ed wants to talk to you, have him do it out loud. Listen closely. What does your Ed sound like? Describe his voice and tone. Let him say what he wants, but come back with positive statements. "Talking back to Ed," with the awareness of him as a separate person, will give you an experience of your own confidence and power.

44

MUSIC

"If I need an extra boost of confidence, or a reminder of the work of recovery, or to hear stories that reflect my reality, I turn to music."

Music is one of my favorite companions. I usually have my music handy on my computer, ipod, car radio, home stereo, or cell phone so I can listen to a song in an instant. If I can't get to any of these, I can often be found humming or singing!

Music gives me so many things: encouragement, support, feelings of joy and release. It helps me through difficult times by connecting me to an inner source of strength. It both relaxes and motivates me. It usually lifts my mood. If I need an extra boost of confidence, or a reminder of the work of recovery, or to hear stories that reflect my reality, I turn to music.

I pick and choose certain songs to help me depending on the situation. As my recovery progresses, I add new ones to my playlist. Here are some that have helped me along my way:

"When You Put Your Heart In It" by Kenny Rogers
"Keep Holding On" by Avril Lavigne
"Life Without Ed" by Jenni Schaefer
"Bye, Bye" by Jo Dee Messina
"Keep the Faith" by Jo Dee Messina
"Believe" by Josh Groban
"This Will Be (Everlasting Love)" by Natalie Cole
"Proud" by Heather Small
"Stronger Woman" by Jewel
"Beautiful" by Christina Aguilera

"Free" by Elliott Yamin
"All I Want To Do" by Sugarland

RECOVERY TOOLS

* Music

REFLECTIONS

What music speaks to you? Listen carefully to one of your favorite songs and see what happens to your mood when the first notes are played. How do you feel when the song is over? Start a "Recovery Boost" playlist of songs that you can listen when you need extra encouragement to keep moving forward.

45

AFFIRMATIONS

"I also repeated my affirmations out loud every day so I would actually hear my voice speak in a kind and positive way."

During recovery, there are many moments when an extra lift of encouragement or positive thought is needed. Reaching out to supports is great, but sometimes they are unavailable. In order to keep myself on track and in the right frame of mind, I decided to carry with me words of encouragement so I could pull them out anytime I needed.

I went to some of my favorite Web sites and printed out some of their affirmations in fun colors. Then I got my index cards, stickers, markers, and tape and went to town by decorating the cards and taping my affirmations to them. Not only was it healing to "absorb" the affirmations while I was working, but the project itself was also relaxing and focused my mind on something positive. Arts and crafts do that for me.

To make sure I had my affirmations around when I needed them, I kept some in my purse, briefcase, car, and at home. Also, since my vehicle takes me everywhere I go, I decided to outfit it with an affirmation, too—a vanity plate! After much thought about what I wanted to communicate to my psyche and the world, I came up with "Bye, bye, Ed." Then, each time I got in and out of my vehicle, I saw that message—a confirmation of my continued commitment to recovery. I read it with pride in my heart and dedication in my soul.

I also repeated my affirmations out loud every day so I would actually hear my voice speak in a kind and positive way. Before I started this practice, someone suggested that I stand in front of a mirror and say the affirmation while looking at myself. But my struggle with a bad body image posed a challenge. Since I did not want this potentially positive tool to turn into a negative one, I thought long and hard about how I could do this without triggering myself at the same time.

Then it came to me: looking into my eyes was more important than looking at my whole body, because the eyes are the windows to my soul. And a loving connection to my soul was what I was after. I pulled out a small hand mirror and took a peek. Lo and behold, I could look deep into my eyes and utter one positive word after another—and it felt good! Like a gift I was giving myself. From that day on, I kept my mirror handy, too.

Here are some of the affirmations I use:

1. I have faith in my process of recovery.
2. I am strong. I have the power. I can decide.
3. One step at a time. That is how I will get where I'm going.
4. I deserve to recover. I am worth it. I can do it.
5. Beat Ed!
6. Food is my friend, not my foe.
7. Do what it takes.
8. I am in the right place at the right time doing the right thing.
9. Believe.
10. The process is worth the reward.
11. Live for the moment.
12. Life is good.
13. Live life, don't just merely exist.

RECOVERY TOOLS

- Affirmations
- Arts and crafts
- Positive self-talk
- Index cards with affirmations
- Saying daily affirmations out loud—sometimes in a mirror

Surrounding yourself with positive thoughts helps when the negative thoughts arise. What are some of your favorite affirmations? Where can you put them so they are accessible to you when you need them? Try beginning each day with an affirmation in the mirror. A positive thought is a powerful tool in your fight for freedom.

46

TRUST

*"I knew I had to take the leap, fight for control,
and trust Bob and Recovery."*

Around this time, Ed was in my face more than usual, and I found myself listening to him here and there. My behaviors did not go unnoticed: Rachel and my treatment team were tuned in to what was happening and were there to support and offer advice.

At one of our sessions, worried that Ed would steal my attention and take me back, Bob mentioned various ways to continue to step in and regain control. He said, "One strong step would be evening treatment, Cheryl."

"I don't need any more treatment," I shot back. "I am totally fine. How much treatment does a person have to do, anyway? I know what I am doing!" Although he voiced his concerns, I told him I wasn't interested, but I would think about it.

"I'll check in with you tomorrow," he said.

The next day I headed home right after work. Rachel wasn't home yet, so it was just me and the dogs. I had the quiet time I needed to think. Rachel and my treatment team were telling me that evening treatment would be a good addition to my recovery, but I wasn't so sure. After all, I was only listening to Ed here and there, which wasn't so bad, right? Wrong!

When the phone rang I knew it was Bob calling to see if I had decided to include evening treatment in my recovery plan.

"Have you thought about what I said?" he asked.

"Yes, and I have decided that I don't need to go to evening treatment," I answered.

"Did you decide that or did Ed?"

"I did. I'm totally fine and you are blowing things way out of proportion. I've had enough treatment already. I don't need it!" I said, my voice rising.

"Cheryl, you've been listening to Ed and you need to trust me. Evening treatment will help you find ways to continue to interrupt the negative behaviors that have been increasing lately," Bob countered.

"You are being unreasonable and unfair; you don't know what you are talking about, and I am fine!" I yelled.

We argued back and forth for a good five minutes and then Bob said something that shook me to my core. "Cheryl, if you are going to continue to listen to Ed and not your support team, then you and I will have to take a break from working together. I am part of *your* team—not Ed's."

His words hit me like a baseball bat to the stomach. I was shocked. With tears in my eyes and a quiver in my voice I asked him, "Are you serious?"

"Yes, I am," he said, sounding like he meant it.

The thought of not having Bob scared me. He had been there with me from the first day of my recovery. *What is going on? What am I doing? Is this really happening?*

Then Ed chimed right in. "Cheryl, you don't need Bob anyway, you only need me. Get rid of Thom too, for that matter, and then we can be together—just the two of us."

But Recovery was waiting in the wings. "Cheryl, listen to Bob. Trust him. He knows how to help you. He is telling you the truth, I promise. Ed is giving you bad advice."

The two of them went back and forth in my mind for a few minutes, and I cried to Bob the entire time. Thoughts were swirling around in my head, and my emotions were out of control. Fortunately, though, Recovery's voice was getting louder and clearer than Ed's. I knew I had to take the leap, fight for control, and trust Bob and Recovery. So I did. I said to Bob "Okay, I trust you. I'll do it. I'll do evening treatment."

We wrapped up our conversation and I hung up the phone. Sitting on the floor, patting the dogs, I thought, it can't hurt. I can only gain more knowledge in my fight against Ed, right?

RECOVERY TOOLS

- Trust
- Talk therapy
- Crying

REFLECTIONS

As you travel the path of recovery, do you find yourself listening to Ed here and there? Has he regained your attention? Be honest with yourself and write down three ways that Ed might still be getting you to cooperate with him. Has a support brought it to your attention? Trust your support, not Ed. What steps will you take next to help fight Ed and keep you on the healthy path?

47

EVENING TREATMENT

"We could pose questions to other patients or to the staff, brainstorm ways to interrupt Ed, or talk about problems or issues we were having. I found that even if I wasn't in the mood to talk, by the end of the group I had gotten totally involved."

Evening treatment took place from 5:30 PM to 8:30 PM three nights a week—Mondays, Tuesdays, and Thursdays. Even as I walked towards the building after work on that first cold night, Ed was begging, "Cheryl, why are you doing this? We don't see each other that often. What's the problem?"

I had to put him in his place. "Ed, I don't want to see you anymore, but you keep coming around once in a while and that's a problem. Just leave me alone."

Evening treatment at Walden was in the same space as day treatment, so I was familiar with the surroundings and the staff. I opened the door to find five other patients anxiously waiting for the session to begin. I went in determined to gain more tools to fight Ed. As I sat down in my chair, I smiled at the others and we exchanged hellos. Soon we were chatting up a storm about our days, our struggles, and the week ahead. It was comfortable right from the start.

Every evening had the same routine: group therapy based on one of two approaches, either cognitive-behavioral therapy (CBT), which focuses on confronting cognitive distortions and changing unhealthy thought patterns, or dialectical behavior therapy (DBT), which incorporates principles of CBT with skills concerning mindfulness, distress tolerance, and emotional regulation. Therapy group was followed by a supervised dinner and a process group.

Once a week, we were weighed (we didn't see the number) and our vital signs were taken. In addition, we met with a social worker to go over any issues or problems we were having. A nutritionist was also available to us if we needed support or had questions regarding our meal plans. We had worksheets to fill out daily regarding the meals we ate offsite and any difficult feelings and issues we were facing.

We were required to bring our dinner, which gave us an opportunity to create a "meal on the go" consistent with our individual plans. It was good practice. We all ate together in the group room where conversation or music was always present. It was a relaxed environment and we all seemed to enjoy our time together. After dinner we usually did something to distract us from the discomfort of having eaten, like playing games, meditating, listening to music, or just chatting.

Then we had a process group, which was basically time for anything we needed. We could pose questions to other patients or to the staff, brainstorm ways to interrupt Ed, or talk about problems or issues we were having. I found that even if I wasn't in the mood to talk, by the end of the group I had gotten totally involved. It was a very interactive and helpful tool.

Evening treatment gave me the extra support I needed in a structured environment where I could connect with others like me. We were all in different stages of recovery, but wanted the same thing—to get rid of Ed. I particularly enjoyed the DBT group, which helped me to push negative thoughts aside so my mind could be quiet and still.

When evening treatment ended, I had more tools, strength, and confidence to fight Ed—and win. And even though he was pretty aggravated and kept trying to get my attention, I felt excited to put what I learned into action.

RECOVERY TOOLS

- Evening treatment
- Talking back to Ed
- DBT
- CBT

- Meal planning
- Support groups
- Music
- Socializing
- Following a meal plan
- Playing games
- Eating with supports

REFLECTIONS

Getting extra treatment support in your fight against Ed can be very powerful. Think about your recovery process. Is Ed standing in front of you at times, preventing you from moving forward? What extra help or support would fit into your recovery plan?

48

RENAME A FEAR

*"Now, when a nudge comes along, I know it means that
my body is functioning properly and communicating with
me about what I need to do for it to heal."*

I remember exactly when and where it happened: a Saturday around 11:00 AM and I was on Erin's massage table. One minute I was relaxed, and the next minute fear and anxiety poured through my body as I experienced something that had not happened in a long while. It was hunger.

At first Ed jumped right in and told me to ignore it, that I was stronger than hunger and all I had to do was listen to him and he would make it go away. I gave him the floor to say all he had to say—and then I put a stop to it.

Ed was lying, and I told him so. I also told him I was not going to listen to him on this. Then I reframed his so-called logic and put it into language that made sense to me in terms of my recovery. I affirmed that hunger is a feeling that "normal" people experience every day and it did not mean I was bad or had done anything wrong. On the contrary, it meant I was doing something right: I was getting healthy.

I knew that hunger pains were going to become part of my every day life, because they would help me learn when and how much to eat. And I didn't want to associate hunger with fear. So in order to quickly and decisively make hunger pains about recovery before Ed could creep in and try to take over, I decided to rename them "recovery nudges," which is a positive, healthy twist on something that is scary for me to feel. In this way, I renamed my fear and took away its power.

Now, when a nudge comes along, I know it means that my body is functioning properly and communicating with me about what I need to do for it to heal. My body *needs* to experience recovery nudges in order to keep me strong, healthy, and on the path of recovery.

RECOVERY TOOLS

- Renaming fears
- Talking back to Ed

REFLECTIONS

What fears are you faced with in your process of recovery? Write them down and then rename them so they have a positive spin. When a fear is replaced with a positive thought, it is not as scary and easier to get through. What might you come up with?

49

GOALS AND STEPS

"I had concrete things to work towards, to visualize as aspects of my new, healthy life. And when I achieved them, I knew I was moving forward and kicking Ed's butt."

During my recovery, I knew I was taking steps forward, but sometimes it felt like I wasn't moving at all. I had a hard time seeing progress when it seemed like I was mostly working on learning to eat and handle difficult feelings. Plus, I wanted to be done already! I wanted recovery *now!*

To help me stay focused on taking positive steps and to see the progress I really *was* making, I created lists of goals for myself: short-term (from one day to two weeks) and long-term (anything over three weeks). Then, to help me achieve those goals, I listed the steps I would need to take to accomplish each one.

Putting it all down on paper made the steps to recovery feel real and within my grasp. Checking off each step to a final goal gave me the inspiration and confidence to keep going. I could see the progress I was making, even if I couldn't feel it. Having a "plan" was especially helpful when Ed would start in on me. I had concrete things to work towards, to visualize as aspects of my new, healthy life. And when I achieved them, I *knew* I was moving forward and kicking Ed's butt. That put a smile on my face!

I utilized my treatment team, friends and family to help me come up with a list of goals, along with the steps necessary to achieve each one. Here is an example of one of my goals and steps I took to get there:

Goal: Eat a fear food

Steps to achieve the goal:

1. With support (from my nutritionist, Amy, and Rachel), make a list of fear foods
2. Pick one fear food and select at which meal or snack (the next day) I will eat it
3. Ask Rachel to come to the grocery store with me
4. Hold, touch, and purchase fear food
5. Prepare fear food with Rachel
6. Write in journal to express feelings before eating
7. Ask Rachel to sit and eat meal with me
8. Use positive self-talk, dogs as a distraction, and conversation during meal
9. Eat and savor fear food
10. Journal, talk to Rachel, and/or call therapist to express feelings around completing the goal
11. Make commitment to complete goal again
12. Success! Yeah!

RECOVERY TOOLS

- Making lists of goals and steps
- Eating a fear food
- Support
- Journaling
- Positive self-talk
- Conversation
- Pets
- Eating with support

Validating your progress in recovery is empowering. Setting goals and achieving them is a great way to see that movement and feel that power. Make a list of goals for your recovery. For example, you might want to make an appointment with a nutritionist or therapist, eat a fear food or 100% of a meal, practice self-care, or buy something for yourself. Then, with a member of your support team (family, friend, or professional) brainstorm on the steps to achieve that goal. Get creative and push yourself. Don't hold back. Then commit to a goal and show Ed you are strong, you don't need him, and you deserve recovery. What will your next step be?

50

PLANNING AHEAD

*"To maintain balance, I also made sure I planned some fun
and relaxation. I booked a sightseeing tour and a massage.
Staying balanced is key. I had a well-rounded trip arranged,
and I was ready to go."*

Being committed to recovery means doing *whatever is necessary, and at this point* I knew it was time to do more intensive
work with Thom. So we set up three consecutive appointments, and I bought a plane ticket to Nashville for my "Trip
Toward Recovery."

From the minute I decided to make the trip, Ed chimed
in, trying to convince me not to go. He even told me I would
get lost, so I should stay home! But no matter how he tried
to maneuver his way in, I stayed determined. *I was worth it!*

Knowing Nashville had lots of recovery help to offer,
I let my fingers do the walking and started planning my
schedule. I found out that Jenni Schaefer was going to be
speaking at a FINDINGbalance (*www.findingbalance.com*)
support meeting on one of the nights I would be in town. I
called, got directions, and told them I would be attending.
I was excited about the prospect of seeing Jenni again and
meeting new people.

Next on my agenda was to find an Eating Disorders
Anonymous (EDA) meeting (*www.eatingdisordersanonymous.
org*), and within seconds of visiting their website, I found a
meeting that would be happening near my hotel. My support groups were all planned out which gave me a sense of
security knowing that I'd be connected to a recovery com-

munity.

To maintain balance, I also made sure I planned some fun and relaxation. I booked a sightseeing tour and a massage. Staying balanced is key. I had a well-rounded trip arranged, and I was ready to go.

RECOVERY TOOLS

- Planning ahead
- Support groups
- Massage
- Fun and relaxation
- Balance

REFLECTIONS

Support groups can be a good way to share feelings, brainstorm, and receive hope with others that understand your struggle. What has been your experience with support groups? If you haven't attended one, why not? Is Ed standing in your way? Would planning ahead make it easier for you? Do a little research and find one to attend.

51

TAKE RISKS

"I knew I had made a lot of headway. I had taken risks, pushed myself, and was moving forward, which felt great. Of course Ed was mad, which I took as a confirmation of my progress!"

On Monday morning I awoke filled with hope and eagerness. *Today is the day I leave for Nashville. By this time tomorrow, I'll be in Thom's office working my butt off.* I got out of bed and went about my normal morning routine: coffee, breakfast, the morning news, and a shower.

I planned on starting my trip off with a bang by having my morning snack at the airport, a bagel and cream cheese (fear foods of mine). After I checked in, allowing plenty of extra time to eat, I proceeded through security and found a Dunkin' Donuts. As I ordered and paid, my heart raced, because I was defying Ed, who called me fat and a loser. He said if I ate the whole thing I wouldn't fit in the seat of the plane. *How stupid does he think I am?*

Sitting near my gate, I pulled out my iPod and prepared my bagel. I took one bite, then another, and while I was listening to music and watching the people milling about, my anxiety gave way to enjoyment. And by the way, the bagel was delicious! After finishing, I texted Bob and told him about my success.

I wish I could say I boarded the plane alone, but Ed came along for the ride, talking the entire time, trying to convince me I didn't know what I was doing and that I would fail. As usual, I told him to button it.

I checked into the hotel and unpacked my suitcase knowing I had a free day ahead of me to explore. I love country music, so being in Music City, USA was a thrill. However, I had to take care of first things first—lunch. Just around the corner, I discovered a sandwich and soup place. Perfect! With nerves of steel I placed my order and grabbed a table by the window to do some more people watching. Most of them were college students from Vanderbilt University, and when I felt tempted to compare bodies, I pulled out my journal and wrote instead.

That evening, with directions in hand, I climbed into a cab and set off for a 20-minute drive to the FINDINGbalance meeting, where I was welcomed with open arms into a warm and comfortable place filled with cozy furniture, burning candles, the smell of coffee, and warm, friendly faces. I quickly felt at ease and safe. Before the meeting began, Jenni and I chatted and laughed, especially when I showed her my new flower tattoo, which had been inspired by her *Life Without Ed*™ jewelry. Soon the program started, and she told her story, which was uplifting. That was followed by an engaging question-and-answer session.

Afterwards, we all talked about our processes, hopes, and dreams. Even as a newcomer, I felt intimately connected to these women with whom I shared the same quest for recovery. All in all, the relaxed atmosphere, group participation, and Jenni's enthusiasm made for a great evening.

I headed back to the hotel with hope and strength running through my veins. What a night! I laid my head on the pillow and smiled as I closed my eyes and clutched Moo Moo. I couldn't wait for the next day to begin.

Tuesday morning came, and I was excited about having my first face-to-face session with Thom. While eating breakfast—room service—the sun came through the window and shone on my back like the embrace of warm arms. Even though I was alone, I felt supported.

I walked to Thom's office, appreciating every step on this road to recovery. When I arrived, I immediately felt hope in my heart. The excitement in my belly was almost unbearable as I took a seat on the sofa in the waiting area. On the end tables were books he had written and various other reading material. The front wall was filled with articles, cartoons, posters, and affirmations.

Within minutes Thom opened a door and greeted me, "Hey Cheryl, how ya doing? Welcome."

Smiling from ear to ear, I stood up and said, "Hi Thom. I'm doing great."

"Let's get started," he said. I followed him into his cozy office and took a seat. I was ready and raring to go. We both were.

The session was intense, but I learned a lot about myself and Ed in just one day. Here are some points from Thom that I took away from that meeting:

- The essence of my relationship with Ed is brainwash.
- Our relationship is one-sided; it's just his way or no way.
- Ed doesn't care about me, he only wants me to do what he says.
- I have to take full responsibility to change this. Don't blame Ed.
- Recovery is strong, firm, tough love. Feel that energy.
- I am not close to perfect; no one is perfect.

I left with homework to do and thoughts about what I had learned about myself during the session. I contemplated the newfound knowledge and the hard work ahead.

Shortly after the session, I came across an old-fashioned diner and stopped in for lunch. As soon as I considered eating any fear foods, Ed quickly interjected that I shouldn't. But Thom's words from our session were louder. I ordered two risk foods—a BLT and an ice cream milkshake. In all honesty, I did experience some guilt and shame, but the meal also felt liberating and was actually yummy. I did a little journaling there, but purposely sat at the counter to engage with other diners and the servers. I didn't isolate. I had disobeyed Ed and gotten what I wanted. I walked back to the hotel with my head held high.

The next two days were full of sessions with Thom, doing homework, eating risk foods, and having a little fun in between. I got the massage I'd booked on one of the days and took the sightseeing tour on the next. I met different people and found out a lot about Nashville and its history. I also confess that a high point of the vacation part of the trip was my visit to the Country Music Hall of Fame.

Of course, it wasn't all fun and games. The sessions with Thom were especially powerful. I taped my sessions and listened to them again later in the day, took notes, and did assignments. Here are some of the messages that came from our second and third sessions:

- Celebrate milestones (like eating risk foods, etc.).
- You are supposed to eat more than your meal plan, which is only a minimum requirement.
- Take ZERO advice from Ed.
- Be prepared. Have a plan.
- Don't be a victim.
- Commit to recovery.
- There are no breaks in recovery.
- Your life is about you, not Ed.
- As you separate from Ed, you gain your own identity.
- You are not Ed.
- Understand "can't" versus "won't."
- Don't debate with Ed.

On my last night in Nashville I went to an Eating Disorders Anonymous meeting, which was only a ten-minute walk from the hotel. In a white house and up a few flights of stairs, I met with a small, intimate group of women, all of whom had one thing in common—defeating Ed. I felt a kindred connection with them. Even in another city, I was surrounded by support.

As I boarded the plane for home the next day, I knew I had made a lot of headway. I had taken risks, pushed myself, and was moving forward, which felt great. Of course Ed was mad, which I took as a confirmation of my progress! My "Trip Toward Recovery" proved that I was stronger than Ed.

RECOVERY TOOLS

- Taking risks
- Talk therapy
- Music
- Eating fear foods in restaurants

- Journaling
- Support groups
- Disobeying Ed
- Self-care
- Massage
- Following a meal plan
- Positive self-talk
- Fun activities

REFLECTIONS

Taking risks shows Ed that you are not afraid and you are in control, not him. Write down five risks that you want to take and three steps that can get you there. What risks have you already taken?

52

PROTECT YOUR
INNER CHILD

"My inner child represents all of my disappointments, hurts, and traumas that I experienced in my early years. By creating a strong, loving parental voice to speak to that part of my self, I could begin the process of healing those wounds."

At one of my sessions with Thom, we talked about how the little girl inside of me still looked up to Ed and admired him. This innocent, inner child didn't realize that Ed was actually like an abusive babysitter and that, in the past, the "adult Cheryl" had left her unprotected.

According to Thom, my inner child represents all the disappointments, hurts, and traumas that I experienced in my early years. By creating a strong, loving, parental voice to speak to that part of my self, I could begin the process of healing those wounds. He said that this would also help me with the process of becoming an independent, self-caring adult.

He explained that we needed to try to enlist the trust of my inner little girl and show her that Ed was not a good companion. She didn't know any better and assumed that he was looking out for her best interests. She believed his lies. To undo Ed's influence and make her feel safe, I had to nurture my inner child with love and guidance.

For homework, Thom asked me to write a letter to my inner child from the adult Cheryl. Before I sat down to write it, I thought about what I wanted to say. I didn't want to scold or try to convince her Ed was bad, because I feared she'd take his side. I was also scared she wouldn't give me a chance, as I had abandoned her so many times before. I just wanted to tell her the truth and hoped that in the end she would develop the confidence that I truly loved her and would be strong enough to protect her. This is what I wrote:

Dear Little Girl,

I am sorry I have not been there for you when you needed me the most. The pain and suffering you have gone through and *are* going through is not your fault. I am here for you now, and I will take you under my wing and protect you for a lifetime. Come with me; you will find strength, happiness, safety, contentment, love, and hope. I will help you fight the lies Ed tells you and will show you the truth. You can count on me to be beside you forever. I won't let you down.

I love you,

Cheryl

Writing this letter helped me experience compassion for myself. It was a powerful way to connect with that innocent girl who was longing for my protection; my words conveyed something she needed to hear and something I needed to say.

RECOVERY TOOLS

- Protecting the inner child
- Honesty
- Writing
- Talk therapy

REFLECTIONS

Think about your relationship with your inner child. How have you let her down, and what are you prepared to do to make things right? Sit in a quiet place and reflect. Listen to what she is saying. What would you like say to her? Write a letter.

53

FACE ED
HEAD ON AT MEALS

"I responded to each of his negative comments with a positive reply and, more important, a bite of food. As I continued to eat, Ed grew quiet. The message was becoming clear: Watch out, here I come!"

When I first began my recovery, I wanted to be as far away from Ed as I could during mealtimes, so I could try to eat in peace. But he just wouldn't leave me alone!

During one of our sessions, Thom, pointed out that I needed to face my fear, and to help with that, he suggested an exercise: *set a place for Ed at the table and have him sit with me while I ate.* This way I could look right at him and tell him with confidence and force who was in charge. I thought that would be hard and scary, but I agreed to give it a shot.

So at my next meal, straight across from me, I set a place for Ed. I gave him a placemat, napkin, plate, knife, fork, and glass. I was nervous because I had no idea how he or I might react. Nevertheless, I fixed my plate and sat down to dinner. There he was, looking right at me with a big smile on his face. He was so smug and so cocky! He thought things were going to be like they used to be. Boy, was he wrong!

Before he could launch into his usual spiel, I said with exaggerated drama, "Ed this food is sooooo good. It's cooked perfectly, and I love it!"

He rolled his eyes at me and said, "You're fooling yourself; you know you shouldn't be eating it. You're going to get fat."

"You have no clue what you're talking about, and frankly, I couldn't care less what you think," I snapped.

While I ate that dinner, I responded to each of Ed's negative comments with a positive reply and, more importantly, a bite of food. As the meal went on, he grew quiet. The message was becoming clear: Watch out, here I come! We were both beginning to realize that he couldn't stop me. He still tried, but I dominated the conversation and the situation. Now *I was* the force to be reckoned with.

As the weeks went by, I continued to set a place for Ed at every meal. But I started to notice his presence diminishing. My strength was overpowering his. He had no reason or desire to sit with me anymore. He had lost his grip and I was in control.

RECOVERY TOOLS

- Facing Ed head on at meals (and dominating)
- Following a meal plan
- Talk therapy

REFLECTIONS

Set a place for Ed at your own table. When you sit down, what will you say to him? What kinds of things does he usually say to you? Write down three positive comebacks that you will use to defend yourself if he tries to keep you from enjoying your meal.

54

CRYING

"By allowing myself to feel my sorrow instead of being numb to it, my recovery got stronger."

Our 14-year-old dog Maxie had cancer. Like anyone who loves their pets, we did all we could for her, including four surgeries to remove tumors from her mouth. She had ups and downs and was still puppy-like at times, but eventually we had to make the very hard decision to let her go. Of course, that day was sad, difficult, and draining. We lost part of our family, and the grief was enormous. A part of me was gone forever.

I wanted to rid my entire being of all the sadness over Maxie's passing, and my thoughts turned to Ed. I knew he could relieve my suffering by making me numb, but at what cost? Running to negative behaviors makes *all* the feelings go away—good ones *and* bad ones. It would be hard, but I wanted to experience the pain, because it would allow me to get in touch with the love I had for poor Maxie. Ed would have taken it all away from me, and I wouldn't let him do that.

So even though I didn't want to, I continued to eat my meals and snacks and felt the anguish with each bite. I cried a lot both for Maxie and myself, and friends and family helped me to express my sorrow. Ed always told me that crying was a sign of weakness, but I was learning that even though it made me vulnerable and raw, that was a much healthier way to face the situation than by running to Ed. I had to remember that feeling sad and crying was okay, as it meant that I could appreciate the depth of my loss and was a sign of progress in my recovery.

I used my journal to get my painful thoughts out. With

my tears falling on the pages, I wrote down memories of Maxie and about my heartache now that she was gone. I also composed a letter in my journal, telling her how much she meant to me. Writing was a way to release all my emotions, both happy and sad, which was gave me a sense of calm and relief.

By allowing myself to feel my sorrow instead of being numb to it, my recovery got stronger. I surely would have regretted spending that precious time with Ed instead of grieving for my beloved companion of so many years.

RECOVERY TOOLS

- Crying
- Talking back to Ed
- Following a meal plan
- Journaling
- Feeling
- Getting support

REFLECTIONS

Learning to cope with difficult feelings is an important part of life and recovery. Crying is a natural and worthwhile way to express sadness and loss. When is the last time you cried? Have you run to Ed to escape? List three tools you can use to deal with feelings in a healthy way.

55

WEIGHT GAIN

"Reaching my goal weight proved that even though I was a bigger size, people still loved and respected me...even more so because they could see how hard I worked to get healthy."

The phone rang on a Friday night, and I could see by caller ID that it was Bob. That seemed unusual, and I felt a little nervous. *What could he want?* I answered with a question, "Hi Bob, is everything okay?"

"I want to check in with you on a few things," he said. Bob and I often talked about my various appointments, as my treatment team was in close email communication with each other so everyone would keep up-to-date on my progress. Bob mentioned my upcoming nutrition appointment with Amy as well as my recent appointment with Dr. G. Then, after a brief pause, he added, "I have some good news, Cheryl; you reached your goal weight." His words hit me like a shot of cold air to the face and my heart skipped a beat. First came fear, then came pride—fear because I knew Ed would be furious and I needed to be ready for him, and pride because I had worked so hard to get there.

After we hung up, I sat for a few moments in stunned silence. I'd gotten rid of my scale months ago and had blind weigh-ins ever since. I suspected that I'd been gaining, but hearing that I'd reached my goal took me by surprise.

Hearing those words—"you reached your goal weight"—was bittersweet. I wanted to be happy and celebrate my accomplishment, but Ed immediately started in. "You are a fat loser and you disappointed me," he said. "All you have to do to get back to normal is do what I say." On some level, I wanted to believe him, but deep down I knew that he could only give me loneliness, depression, feelings of worthlessness, and other equally painful feelings. I no longer wanted what he offered, and I told him so.

"Ed, I'm not listening. You don't know what's best anymore. Go away. I am proud that I reached this goal, and nothing you say will change that." When Ed got mad, I knew that it meant that my recovery was getting stronger.

Reaching my goal weight actually gave me a sense of power and freedom. It proved that I could overcome Ed's influence and live without him. It also proved that even though I was a bigger size, people still loved and respected me...even more so because they could see how hard I worked to get healthy. I even began to respect myself. The extra weight also helped my mind and body function properly, which was crucial for fully participating in each day and accomplishing goals I set. It was a paradox: even though the weight was hard to accept at times, I felt healthier and more nourished inside and that kept me going. Being a bigger size wasn't detrimental to my life—it enhanced it.

RECOVERY TOOLS

- Weight gain
- Talking back to Ed

REFLECTIONS

What thoughts and feelings are you faced with by weight gain? Does it make you anxious, scared, proud, or driven? Write about these feelings in your journal.

56

A WORKOUT BUDDY

"I also hired a personal trainer to come to my house and give me guidance. She knew about my background and concentrated my program more on strength training than aerobics, which used to be my consuming passion.

When I began my recovery, Dr. G. prohibited me from exercising, because I always tended to overdo it. Once I reached a healthy weight, though, she gave me the go-ahead to start up again. I wanted to be able to exercise in moderation for optimal health instead of using it obsessively for weight loss. So, I knew I needed a plan.

On the days I went to the gym, I brought someone along for support—a workout buddy. She showed me how much exercise was appropriate, kept me focused, and provided camaraderie. Having someone knowledgeable who could make suggestions about my routines and movements gave me confidence that I was doing the right things for my body.

I also hired a personal trainer to come to my house and give me guidance. She knew about my background and concentrated my program more on strength training than aerobics, which used to be my consuming passion. She also helped me choose a variety of workout videos, which I could follow on my own. This worked particularly well, because when the video ended, I knew it was time to stop.

Taking a yoga class was another tool I used to control the urge to overexercise. It was just the right amount of exercise for the day. Plus it pushed me to socialize and make new friends. I loved going to yoga class!

So, by having a plan in place, I exercised in healthy moderation and successfully stayed away from working out too much or for the wrong reasons. Balance was key—in both recovery and life.

RECOVERY TOOLS

- Workout buddy
- Personal trainer
- Video
- Yoga
- Socializing

REFLECTIONS

Is overexercise a problem for you? What can you do to develop a moderate approach? What types of timed exercise appeal to you? Get help designing a program that will be healthy and fun. Before you begin, be sure to get the okay from your doctor.

57

GRATITUDE
JOURNAL

"I started a gratitude journal. Each night, I wrote down five things for which I felt grateful. They didn't have to be major, but had to be somehow meaningful to me, things that spoke to my heart."

Early in my recovery, when my life was consumed by the constant battling with Ed, I didn't appreciate my life or the people in it. With his words and rules constantly rolling around in my head, I had a hard time even seeing the outside world. I had tunnel vision—Ed vision—and needed to find a way to focus on the positive.

To help me do that, I started a gratitude journal. Each night, I wrote down five things for which I felt grateful. They didn't have to be major, but had to be somehow meaningful to me, things that spoke to my heart. They could be occurrences, exchanges, sights I saw, or words I—or someone else—said. In doing this exercise, I was hoping to find value and meaning in my daily life instead of giving so much attention to Ed.

Here are the five things I wrote down on the first night I did this exercise:

1. I am grateful for Rachel and our time together.
2. I am grateful for my job and co-workers.
3. I am grateful for having been so honest in the conversation I had with my sister-in-law.
4. I am grateful that I got to see a Mother Duck and her babies play together.
5. I am grateful for the great parking spot I got today.

I made this a nightly assignment, and always re-read what I'd written. This helped me realize that I could focus my energy on the good things around me instead of the things Ed wanted me to see. Keeping this gratitude journal gave me a new appreciation for my life and more reasons to disobey Ed!

RECOVERY TOOLS

- Gratitude Journal

REFLECTIONS

At the end of the day, sit down and reflect on your day and what you appreciate about it. Write down five things you are grateful for. Re-read what you write to feel the positive energy. What happened throughout your day today?

58

POSITIVE SELF-TALK

*"I was used to hiding my body, and as I looked at myself, nega-tive thoughts jumped into my mind—but so did positive ones. I liked the way the outfit fit my new body and was happy with what I saw. So I said to myself, **Damn, I look good!**"*

On a Saturday afternoon, I headed to the mall with a Tiffany's gift card burning a hole in my pocket. After picking out two silver rings, I found myself standing in front of an Ann Taylor store pondering whether or not to go in.

Usually, trying on clothes gives me anxiety, bordering on panic and despair. Ed has an opinion about every outfit, and my poor body image often stopped me from actually buying anything. Guilt also played a part, as I often felt unworthy of nice things and gave up. But recovery was changing me. In spite of strong doubts, I said to myself, *I can do this. I deserve it.* After all, having reached my goal weight, I needed some new clothes.

I walked around the store, grabbing various sizes of one item after another, all the while saying to myself, *I'm worthy, I deserve nice things.* With plenty of choices to start with, I head-ed to the dressing room, but when the door shut behind me, I was suddenly aware that my heart was pounding. I got through the moment by taking a few deep breaths and reassuring my-self. *You can do this.* I put one foot in and then the other, as I pulled the pants up my bare legs, past my hips to my waist.

For a few moments, I stood alone in that secluded dressing room, but realized that I couldn't stop there. So I said out loud, "Let's do this," and I took the plunge: I stepped outside of my safe cubicle and stood in front of the public, three-sided mirror.

I was used to hiding my body, and as I looked at myself, negative thoughts jumped into my mind—but so did positive ones. I liked the way the outfit fit my new body and was happy with what I saw. So I said to myself, *Damn, I look good.*

Then a sales assistant came over, and we talked about my tastes. A few minutes later she came back with more items for me to consider. I felt a bit overwhelmed, but I appreciated her help. I liked having someone else's opinion—other than Ed's—about what actually looked good on me. So I took the stack into the dressing room and began the task of trying it all on.

At one point, I came out wearing a beautiful, gold, cashmere sweater and gray, dress pants. I liked the overall look, but thought the pants were too tight. I wasn't used to wearing anything that actually fit, so this was a new concept for me! But the sales person came over and said, "You look great. That outfit fits you perfectly." I expressed that they felt snug, but she disagreed. I did the sitting down and bending test and logically they did seem to be okay. I was learning!

I tried on other outfits, all the while feeling good about myself. I looked at my body from various angles and did not judge as much as I had in the past. Don't get me wrong, Ed still lurked in the background with his trash talking, but I had better things to do than listen to him.

After I finished picking out what I liked, the guilt began to emerge. To take control of the situation and have a reality check, I stayed in the dressing room and worked on my positive self-talk. *You've worked hard to gain this weight and get healthy. You deserve to reward yourself with something new!*

I was learning to live in the moment and in that particular one, I felt good about myself. So I took that feeling and ran with it. I gathered my stuff, stepped up to the register, and had the cashier ring me up. Incidentally, I bought those pants and have worn them many times!

RECOVERY TOOLS

- Positive self-talk
- Deep breathing
- Talking back to Ed

REFLECTIONS

How do you feel about clothes shopping? Is it the time in your recovery for some new outfits? Take someone with you on a shopping trip, and plan it in advance. Where will you go? What do you need? Be sure to buy something! Afterwards, write in your journal about how you felt before, during, and after.

59

BODY CHEER

"Is my cheer silly? Sure, it's quirky and won't win a Grammy! But it helps me through difficult times. It states a truth I need to keep hearing: My body is beautiful, and so am I!"

As my body was changing and becoming healthier, I wanted something positive to say each time I saw myself in a negative light or was having a bad body image day. So I decided to come up with a body cheer. I figured that saying (or singing) it over and over would help lift me up when I was feeling down. So armed with paper and pen, I got to work.

The exercise was a success. Not only did I come up with a rally cry, but the project itself also kept my thoughts focused on recovery instead of the "sing song" of Ed's voice. I enjoyed the challenge, and here's what I came up with:

I love my body, oh yes, I do,
I love my body, and it is true.
B-O-D-Y, body, body you rock the sky.
B—beautiful
O—outstanding
D—dedicated
Y—you
Go body, go body, go body!

Is my cheer silly? Sure, it's quirky and won't win a Grammy! But it helps me through difficult times. I sing it when poor body image thoughts race through my mind and I need a little encouragement. It states a truth I need to keep hearing: My body is beautiful, and so am I!

RECOVERY TOOLS

- Body cheer
- Positive self-talk
- Writing

REFLECTIONS

Saying positive cheers pushes the negative thoughts aside. Write out a personal, uplifting little song that will help you get through low moments. Start writing and humming, and see what pops into your head.

60

SELF-LOVE

"Knowing that people I loved and respected would tell me the truth gave their words that much more power and grounded me in a new reality: I was a good person, and I could learn to love myself."

For my entire life, Ed called me fat and told me how I should feel, and I believed him. I hardly had any self-respect with his demanding and demeaning words floating around in my head all the time. As my recovery progressed, members of my treatment team told me—and I knew deep down—that I had to *learn* how to love and respect myself. So, one day as I meditated, I set an intention to find ways to do that.

As the days went by, several ideas came to me, and I started putting them into action. But at one point I decided to write down everything I could think of that was a reflection of who I am in my heart at the deepest level: compassionate, a good listener, honest, hard working, loyal, giving, witty and many more good things. Seeing this list of what I value made me realize who "I" am apart from Ed, which gave me direction and confidence. It reminded me that I am worthy of love, not only from others, but also from myself.

To help me stay focused on the practice of self-love, I began repeating a mantra, "I give people my heart, respect, and love. I deserve to give those gifts to myself." Even if I didn't fully accept what I was saying, I knew if I kept saying it, I would eventually believe it…even if just a little.

Another idea I had took a lot of courage and was hard to do, but it was quite effective. First, I came up with a list of people that I trusted. Then I asked each of them to tell me three things they liked about me. I wrote down what they said and read it over to myself every morning. I also wrote those positive attributes on an index card, which I kept in my purse and referred to from time to time. Knowing that people I loved and respected would tell me the truth gave their words that much more power and grounded me in a new reality: I was a good person, and I could learn to love myself.

As each day passed, viewing myself with love and respect got a little easier. This new way of thinking didn't come naturally to me after all of Ed's brainwashing. At first, it felt uncomfortable and awkward putting so much time into thinking about "me." My self-praise was often tinged with guilt, as if I didn't deserve to love myself. But I knew the negativity was coming from Ed, and that realization only pushed me to work harder at my recovery.

RECOVERY TOOLS

- Self-love
- Meditation
- Mantras
- Asking for feedback
- Listing and reading positive attributes

REFLECTIONS

Self-love is vital to a lasting recovery. Begin by writing down what you appreciate about yourself. Next, make a list of people you trust and respect. Ask each of them to tell three (or more) things they admire about you. Write down what they say and read them daily or at various times for strength and reflection. You might think it would be hard to hear wonderful things about yourself from other people, but their words will help you learn to love the most important person of all—yourself.

61

TRANSFORM ED'S RULES

"Through this process, I could "see" recovery start to play out right in front of me. And when I read my new statements—after Ed's old rules—I knew I had the ability to make them a reality."

Ed had specific rules for me to follow. He convinced me that if I always did what he instructed, I would be happy, successful, loved—and thin. No matter what situation I was faced with, he always had an answer. Even if the same scenario came up again and again, I had to listen closely because he might have changed the rules. You can imagine how exhausting this was; it took all of my time and concentration to be sure I did everything "right."

Thom suggested transforming Ed's rules into affirmations of recovery. He gave me an example and I told him I would give it a try. He told me not to get discouraged if it took some time to think this through, but my recovery depended upon my invalidating Ed's rules.

So, one afternoon I wrote some down. *These are the rules. How can they be something else?* I remembered Thom's example and, putting my nose to the grindstone, I transformed each rule from a negative to a positive. This took some time and practice, but after I got going, I got the hang of it.

Here are some of Ed's rules and how I reframed and transformed them into recovery statements:

Ed's rule: You must eat less than everyone else.
Reframed: I eat until I am full and satisfied.

Ed's rule: When you go out to a restaurant, only order safe foods.
Reframed: When I go out to a restaurant, order what I want and crave.

Ed's rule: If you weigh enough to give blood, then you are fat and unlovable.
Reframed: If I weigh enough to give blood, then I am healthy enough to help people.

Ed's rule: If you eat bad foods, you must restrict.
Reframed: There is no such thing as bad foods.

Ed's rule: Your skinny clothes must always be too big for you.
Reframed: My clothes will fit my new body, and I will look and feel beautiful.

Ed's rule: If you are in recovery, you are not special or unique anymore.
Reframed: If I am in recovery, I am strong and free.

Ed's rule: If you have your period, it means you are too fat.
Reframed: Having my period means my body is working properly and I am healthy.

Through this process, I could "see" recovery start to play out right in front of me. And when I read my new statements—after Ed's old rules—I knew I had the ability to make them a reality. With every transformation I wrote, Ed's power was diminishing, and I was getting stronger.

RECOVERY TOOLS

- Transforming Ed's rules
- Persistence
- Talk therapy
- Practice

REFLECTIONS

Sit in a quiet place armed with your journal or a piece of paper. Think about the rules that Ed has for you and write them down. Look at them one by one and transform each rule into a reflection of your recovery statement. Don't give up; be persistent. When you are done, read your new statements back to yourself and feel the power behind them.

62

THROW AWAY YOUR SKINNY CLOTHES

"Every thought and feeling attached to those clothes was connected to the misery and despair of unattainable goals. I was aiming something different—the health and happiness that comes with recovery."

When I would get dressed, I used to walk into my closet and grab something off the rack. In the process, I would look aimlessly at all my clothes, my eyes lingering on the top shelf—the one that held my skinny clothes. I used to reminisce about wearing them and fantasize about what life was like when I was thinner.

One day I caught myself looking at the top shelf and realized that those clothes and the feelings surrounding them were still taking up space in my mind and heart. Ed hoped that someday I would fit into them again. But I knew that would never, and could never, happen without a complete return to my eating disorder—and I certainly did not want that. Still, having them gave me a sense of comfort and hope, albeit in the wrong direction.

In order to continue to move ahead in my recovery, I knew I had to part with those clothes and get rid of their bad karma. So the next weekend I armed myself with a large trash bag and headed to the closet. To help me with this difficult task, I brought along a few items of comfort: a cup of coffee, my favorite country music station, Moo Moo, my stuffed cow, and my orange giraffe.

Of course, Ed chimed right in and said, "Cheryl, this is a mistake. You can get back into those clothes. Just listen to me; it can happen. I know you can do it. I have faith in you." I listened to what he was telling me and then snapped back, "That's enough, Ed. I'm fine on my own. I don't need you, but thanks anyway." I stayed firm, so he knew I meant business.

Before placing each item into the bag, I held it and remembered the rules and feelings associated with it. I was a bit sad at first because I knew I would never be that size again, but I quickly realized that *I didn't want to be that size again.* Every thought and feeling attached to those clothes was connected to the misery and despair of unattainable goals. I was aiming for something different—the health and happiness that comes with recovery. So one by one I said good-bye to each piece, and felt hopeful and excited for all that lay ahead. Pieces of the old Cheryl were gone as the real Cheryl took a stand for freedom.

RECOVERY TOOLS

- Throw away your skinny clothes
- Tangible objects
- Music
- Talking back to Ed

REFLECTIONS

Have you gotten rid of your skinny clothes yet? What's holding you back? Would you donate them, cut them up, or throw them out with the garbage? Grab a bag and head for your closet!

63

DISOBEY ED

"Even though Ed told me I didn't have to eat since I was seasick, I told him that that rule didn't apply, and I had to eat anyway. My treatment team would have been proud."

Rachel and I booked a cruise to the Caribbean, and I was ready to get away and relax. On our flight, though, I realized that Ed had come along—not sitting next to me, but in the last row. At the time, my excitement and the drone of the engines made it easy to ignore him.

We spent a few days in Florida visiting with my in-laws before the cruise. They showed us around, and we ate in some cool restaurants. We had a fun and relaxing time so the vacation was off to a great start.

Unfortunately, once our ship left the dock, the seas were rough and the boat rocked and swayed non-stop. Seasickness took hold and would not let up—even though I wore a prevention patch. I was often nauseous and had a splitting headache. Curling up in a ball on the bed was almost a daily occurrence.

Ed sensed what was going on and wanted to take advantage of the situation. "Cheryl, stop eating and you'll start to feel better." I told him I wouldn't listen to his nonsense. *Does he think I'm going to fall for that? Being seasick has nothing to do with him!* I knew for sure that I had to force some nourishment into my body to feel better. Yet, Ed could be incredibly persistent and annoying, especially when I felt lousy.

So, I decided that listening to Ed was not an option. Despite the fact I wasn't feeling well, I had to stick to my meal plan. Otherwise, he wouldn't leave me alone. He laughed at me, but I didn't care. I wanted the vacation to be without him, and I was angry that he came along for the ride! Days went by and I regularly ate meals, snacks, and even fear foods. Even though Ed told me I didn't have to eat since I was seasick, I told him that that rule didn't apply, and I had to eat anyway. My treatment team would have been proud.

By the end of the cruise, I felt empowered. I had acknowledged that Ed was tagging along, but I always disobeyed him. I knew what would make me feel better, not him. I stayed true to my recovery and even managed to have a good time. Despite the seasickness, the vacation was a success! And I wore a bathing suit! Success times two!

RECOVERY TOOLS

- Disobeying Ed
- Following a meal plan
- Fun activities
- Distraction
- Family
- Going out to eat
- Eating with supports

REFLECTIONS

Is Ed whispering in your ear right now? Write down what he is telling you, and then push back and write down your recovery response. Actively disobey him. If he is telling you not to eat something, eat it. Do the opposite of what Ed is telling you. By doing so, you take your power back and diminish his.

64

RECOVERY
WEB SITES

"I found some favorite sites and read other people's stories, participated in chats, or followed blogs. Browsing these sites gave me the extra comfort of knowing I was not alone."

Even though I surrounded myself with supports and items to help my recovery, sometimes I still wanted a little bit more—something extra. That's when I turned to the Internet where I found some favorite sites and read other people's stories, participated in chats, or followed blogs. Browsing these sites gave me the extra comfort of knowing I was not alone in my journey and confirmed everything I was going through in recovery. Here are a few helpful sites:

Gürze Books (eating disorders information and resources, publisher of this book)
www.bulimia.com

Eating Disorder Blogs (over a dozen ED bloggers; also from Gürze Books)
www.eatingdisordersblogs.com

My ED Help (online recovery community)
www.myedhelp.com

Thom Rutledge (psychotherapist, author of **Embracing Fear**, and coauthor of **Life Without Ed**)
www.thomrutledge.com

Andrea Roe (survivor and author of **You Are Not Alone, Volumes 1 and 2**)
www.youarenotalonebook.com

Shannon Cutts (survivor, author of *Beating Ana*, and founder of Key-to-Life and MentorCONNECT)
www.mentorconnect-Ed.org

Jenni Schaefer (survivor and author of *Goodbye Ed, Hello Me* and *Life Without Ed*)
www.jennischaefer.com

Something Fishy (eating disorders information, support, and forums)
www.somethingfishy.org

National Eating Disorders Association (largest non-profit organization devoted to eating disorders)
www.nationaleatingdisorders.org

My Self Help (general health and wellness)
www.myselfhelp.com

FINDINGbalance (faith-based organization devoted to eating disorders)
www.findingbalance.com

RECOVERY TOOLS

- Web sites

REFLECTIONS

When you want and need that something extra for support, where do you go to find it? Realizing you are not alone in your thinking or fight is comforting. Visit some of the websites I've listed.

65

PUT DISTANCE BETWEEN YOU AND ED

"Being able to see a kind of physical separation between us was key to my recovery. I was willing to coexist in the same house, but I wanted to keep the doors up between us."

In all the years that Ed dominated my life, I usually imagined him right next to me (on my left side). Sometimes he sat on my lap and even got on my back. He knew exactly where to position himself to be most disruptive.

As my recovery progressed, Ed shifted. At first, he was pretty ticked at me so he didn't want to leave my side. But over time, he started to walk a step or two behind me—a sign of progress.

At one point further on in my recovery, I used a psychological construct to put Ed in his place. I envisioned a structure in my mind—my "house"—made up of several rooms on one floor. This is where Ed lived. There were no doors, but there was enough space for us to be apart from each other. When I told Ed to leave me alone, he would go off into a distant room. Sure, he came back to see if I would follow him—but our relationship was changing.

As more time went on, I added a second floor to my "house" and put up doors. Then, instead of just telling Ed to leave, I told him to "go upstairs" further away from me. This way, even though Ed and I still lived together, we were separated by doors, walls, and floors.

Eventually, Ed would only rarely come into the same room I was in, and even then his talking became softer. Usually, he'd stay away upstairs, shut in, his voice muffled or practically nonexistent.

Being able to envision a physical separation between us was key to my recovery. I was willing to coexist in the same house, but I wanted to keep the doors up between us. I could tell him to go away and be specific; he'd hear me and leave. Definite progress!

RECOVERY TOOLS

- Putting distance between you and Ed
- Talking back to Ed

REFLECTIONS

Where does your Ed reside? Where is he right now? Create distance between you and Ed. Put him in another room or on an island. Think about where he would go. Has his position changed as you have moved forward in your recovery?

66

END THE
CONVERSATION

"In the past, I talked back, but Ed always left with a part-
ing remark. I discovered that I could take my power back by
interrupting him each time with a variety of recovery-based
activities. That put an end to the conversation!"

I suppose everyone wakes up on the wrong side of the bed
from time to time. That happened to me one day, and I was
in a bad funk and not particularly optimistic. I wavered back
and forth about whether I even wanted recovery. Feeling hopeless and helpless, thoughts raced through my mind like, *I am*
never going to get through this. As I battled with uncertainty and
depression, Ed tried to win me over, "Cheryl, all you need to
do to feel better is to restrict. You don't need recovery. All you
need is me."

Even in my vulnerable state, Ed's words weren't sitting
well, so I repeated a positive mantra to drown them out. But
as the day progressed, the dark clouds remained and my bad
body image took hold. Ed kept pressing, "You know, your
treatment team is a disgrace. They betrayed you and made you
get fat. I won't let you down like they did."

With that remark, I knew I had a decision to make: Would
I listen to what Ed was telling me, or would I push ahead with
my recovery? Then the thought came to me: *I can turn this*
around! I let Ed finish what he had to say, and then I yelled,
"Ed, go to your room and leave me alone. I refuse to have this
conversation with you!"

I had to take control and put a plan in action to keep myself safe. First, I needed to reconnect with my body, so I took

myself to a yoga class. That allowed me get into a quiet place and do something respectful of my body—to experience it as the temple it is. Yoga also helped me direct my fear, insecurities, and anxiety outward so my mind would be clear and still. Then, I could let everything go and just relax.

Dinner came next. To show Ed I was in control, I made a fear food. I also fed my dogs, and we all ate together in front of the TV—and I enjoyed every bite. While I cleaned the dishes, I turned on the radio and sang out loud to push Ed out of my mind. The dogs were howling as my voice got louder and louder. Thank goodness no one could hear us!

My mood had picked up considerably, and although he wanted to come out, Ed was still in his room. To finish the night off with a bang, I logged on to Voice America's Web site and listened to Doris Smeltzer's show, *Savor Yourself...Beyond Skin Deep*. Hearing her wisdom about recovery was comforting, soothing, and empowering (archives of the show can be found at *www.andreasvoice.org*).

As the day came to an end, I felt good! I had indeed turned the day around and was proud of myself for not letting Ed have the last word. In the past, I talked back, but he always left with a parting remark. I discovered that I could take my power back by interrupting him each time with a variety of recovery-based activities. That put an end to the conversation!

RECOVERY TOOLS

- Ending the conversation
- Talking back to Ed
- Positive mantra
- Yoga
- Following a meal plan
- Distraction (TV)
- Music
- Recovery web sites
- Pets
- Eating a fear food

Ending the conversation with Ed shows strength and proves to him you are taking your power back. Write down five things you can do to end a conversation with Ed and keep them close at hand so you can use them when needed. As Thom always told me, "Never let Ed get the last word. It is important that *you* have the last word."

67

MEALS TO GO

"I had yummy leftovers in the fridge from the night before and packed them in a container. Ed said I'd look stupid, 'Everyone will be staring at you.' But I didn't care."

I had plans to head over to the local park after work to see my niece Stephanie play softball. This particular game was being held at a field without a concession stand, which posed a dilemma: *What was I going to do for dinner?* Predictably, Ed told me I could miss one meal. "Not a big deal," he said.

I knew better. Skipping a meal was not an option, because it would be an invitation for Ed to take advantage of me and as I learned from Thom, there are no breaks in recovery. I thanked Ed for the suggestion, but told him I had a better solution— bringing dinner with me. I had yummy leftovers in the fridge from the night before and packed them in a container. I grabbed silverware and napkins and was ready to go. Ed said I'd look stupid, "Everyone will be staring at you." But I didn't care.

Familiar faces were gathered around and hellos were exchanged. Everyone was having fun. My niece made some nice plays and was clearly enjoying herself. Eventually, I reached into my bag and pulled out my dinner. As I prepared my meal, people did look to see what I was doing.

"My dinner," I said calmly.

Some turned up their noses to get a whiff of what I had brought, and others commented on how tasty it looked and what a good idea it was to bring food. They were hungry! And they were impressed, while I happily ate and watched the game.

My plan had worked perfectly. I stuck to my meal plan,

and no one made fun of me, as Ed said they would. In fact, they were jealous!

RECOVERY TOOLS

- Meals to go
- Talking back to Ed
- Following a meal plan
- Family
- Friends
- Distraction (softball game)

REFLECTIONS

Social events are not an excuse to skip meals. If you wanted to bring a meal with you somewhere—a picnic, potluck, or ball game—what would you bring? Write down a few ideas for meals to go (according to your meal plan) in case you need them.

68

A LETTER TO ED

"I felt tremendous freedom after writing this letter. It was liberating to get the anger out and finally direct it toward the appropriate place. I knew right then I did not have to be angry with myself anymore."

During one of my sessions in Nashville with Thom, we role-played: I played Ed and Thom played me. This exercise allowed me to view myself more objectively, from an outside point-of-view. "We" conversed for quite awhile, and afterwards Thom asked what I thought.

I told him that Ed sounded desperate and full of contradictions. Then, something unexpected happened. I started to feel pure anger toward Ed. My hands turned to fists and I could feel a fire raging inside my belly. Previously, my anger was directed at myself for being weak and listening to Ed. But on that day, he infuriated me. *How dare he treat me that way. Who does he think he is?* I could feel the fury deep down in my soul, only this time it was directed at the correct recipient—Ed.

For homework, to work off that rage, Thom suggested I write an angry letter. He said to let it all out and really let Ed have it. So, I sat on the grass in a park across from my hotel where birds were chirping and the sun warmed my back. The setting could not have been more serene or in greater contrast to the emotions I wanted to express. This is what I wrote:

Dear Ed,

You are not going to like what I have to say, but shut up and listen. I am angry, very angry with you, and it is real. For my entire life, I've shown my commitment to you, and you pulled the wool over my eyes all the while. You lied and manipulated me, and caused me misery. It is only now that I am away from you that I can see that you don't care about me at all. You only care about yourself, the power and the control. You sicken me, and I want to be far away. To even look at you makes me feel sick inside. All those years you told me you cared about me and wanted me to be happy were a lie. You call me a lowlife and a loser if I don't listen, but that's not true. You wouldn't know happiness, success, or freedom if it slapped you across the face. I am angry at how you treated me, and the control you took. I am pissed off and I hate you. All you have ever done is take, take, take. You've given me nothing good— ever. You are full of crap and are nothing to me. I hope you live in the same hell you have put me through.

Good-bye,
Cheryl

I felt tremendous freedom after writing this letter. It was liberating to get the anger out and finally direct it toward the appropriate person. I knew right then I did not have to be angry with myself anymore.

RECOVERY TOOLS

- Writing a letter to Ed
- Role-playing
- Intrapersonal therapy
- Nature

REFLECTIONS

Directing anger away from ourselves and onto Ed is healing and appropriate. Write a letter to Ed and tell him how you feel about him and what he has done. Put all your feelings out there for him to hear. Don't hold back.

69

MINDFUL AT MEALTIMES

"Through the use of positive self-talk, supports, distractions, and having faith in the process, mealtimes had become much more palatable—even enjoyable, at times."

Night after night I went along with my meal plan, and all was fine until at one point I began feeling extremely full and bloated during dinner. Sometimes I had to literally force myself to finish eating. My stomach was uncomfortable, and I was confused. *Why now, after all this time, am I feeling like this? Is Ed trying to sneak in and take over?*

In the beginning stages of recovery, struggling to get through a meal sometimes took hours. But through the use of positive self-talk, supports, distractions, and having faith in the process, mealtimes had become much more palatable—even enjoyable, at times. So, I began to look more carefully at my physical sensations while I ate.

One night, partway through my meal, a large burp bubbled up and I felt an immediate release that gave me more room for food. I continued to eat and drink, and shortly thereafter the uncomfortable feeling came over me again. Rather than panic or revert to an old Ed behavior, I pushed onward while being mindful and paying attention to my body to help solve the mystery.

As I brought the sparkling water to my mouth, my eyes happened to glance at the bottle—and then it came to me like a slap in the back of the head! *It's the carbonation!* I immediately switched to regular water and finished my meal.

The next night I poured myself plain water with dinner.

There I sat, eating my meal, drinking my water, and feeling no ill effects. The feelings of bloating and fullness were not present. I had figured it out! I continued the test for the next few nights and confirmed: no more bubbles during dinner!

RECOVERY TOOLS

- Mindfulness
- Positive self-talk
- Distractions
- Eating with supports
- Following a meal plan

REFLECTIONS

Are you finding it difficult to get through meals? Be mindful and aware, both internally and externally. Check in with yourself. Is your body trying to tell you something?

70

WHO'S TALKING— ED OR ME?

"When I thought about it, I realized that I usually did the talking and was no longer ordering based on caloric value or Ed's old rules."

All through recovery I'd been taught various ways to resist Ed. One was by making food choices based on what *I* wanted, not him. But I noticed that as I leaned toward "healthier" choices rather than risky ones, I would get scared and begin questioning myself. *Was I ordering food based on caloric value again? Was I doing something wrong?*

So at my next session with Thom, I asked, "Am I always supposed to pick the more radical food choice to prove that I am in recovery? Should I be concerned about ordering 'healthier' meals?"

He assured me that I do not always have to order a risky meal to prove anything. He also said I should ask myself, "Who's talking?" In other words, when deciding what to eat, I needed to be sure that *I* was making the choice, not Ed. I had to be true to myself and answer honestly. And when I thought about it, I realized that I really *was* doing more of the talking and no longer ordering based on caloric value or Ed's old rules.

I also needed to give myself a pat on the back. Even though recovery was becoming more mainstream in my life, I was still learning to trust myself, and my wants and desires, because I had always done what Ed wanted. I guess I just needed to be reassured that this brief fear was just part of the recovery process—and it was.

RECOVERY TOOLS

- Asking who's talking—Ed or me
- Talk therapy
- Honesty
- Trust

REFLECTIONS

Think about the last time you made a food choice. Did you make the choice based on what you wanted or what Ed wanted you to pick? Be true to yourself and recovery and answer honestly.

71

PUNCH A PILLOW

"Whenever poor body image days arose, I knew how to deal with them. I recognized what was happening to me, stepped aside, utilized some tools, and got through it."

I woke up in a pretty good mood. I had a cookout to go to in the evening and was excited about seeing friends and meeting new people. I decided to lie down and take a nap in the afternoon so I would be rested for the late night ahead. When it was time to get ready, I made some coffee and jumped in the shower. My mood still seemed fine and nothing was off kilter or out of the ordinary—until I got dressed.

Then the bad body image thoughts took over: I put on an outfit, looked in the mirror, and didn't like what I saw. Starting at my head and going all the way to my toes, I picked apart everything in between. Off came that outfit and on went another, but the self-criticism remained. My insides were churning while I filled up with anger and self-disgust.

When I realized what was happening, I immediately walked away from the mirror. To center myself and get out all those negative feelings, I headed to the bed and grabbed my pillow. Lifting it high over my head, I swung it down really hard onto the bed a few times. Then I began punching it over and over until I felt done, ready to calm myself with some deep breathing. I also held Moo Moo while I counted to fifty and sang a few rounds of my body cheer.

After ten minutes using these various self-soothing tools, I said aloud, "I am not fat and my clothes fit me great. No matter what I put on, I'll be okay." Then I picked out an outfit and got dressed—this time without looking in the mirror—which I knew had been triggering.

While in the car, I sang my body cheer again, listened to music, did positive self-talk, and talked to Rachel to be more upbeat. I did not want the bad thoughts to have power over me. I wanted to be in charge of my mood!

We got to the party and the night went off without a hitch. I enjoyed hanging out and laughing with my friends. People actually commented on my clothes and said how nice I looked. That was a true reality check!

After that, when I was faced with poor body image days, I knew what to do. I recognized what was happening to me, stepped aside, utilized some tools, and turned them around. Learning to love and take care of my body was part of recovery, even though it might take some effort!

RECOVERY TOOLS

- Punching a pillow
- Body cheer
- Deep breathing
- Counting to fifty
- Tangible object
- Positive self-talk
- Talking with supports
- Music
- Friends

REFLECTIONS

Do negative feelings come to the surface when you look in the mirror? If so, how do you release them? Try punching a pillow! Also, think of three positive things you can say about yourself the next time you look in the mirror, like "I am beautiful, and I love and respect my body." Write them down—even if you don't believe them. The next time you face the mirror, say all of them. Matter of fact, do this every day!

72

TATTLE ON ED

"I brought up Ed's tactic and how annoying he was being. Tattling on him was a great recovery tool! Acknowledging his influence to someone else really ticked Ed off and took away his power."

One morning as I started to get dressed, Ed came out of his room and stood right in front of me. As I pulled my pants up to my waist and fastened the button, he said in a soft, soothing, almost comforting voice that my left leg was bigger than my right. This was because I had eaten some food he didn't approve of the previous day and had a filling breakfast that morning.

In hushed tones, he whispered, "Cheryl, what are you doing? Have you forgotten everything I've been telling you? Listen to me now, this is proof. Can you feel your left leg? See, your pants don't feel the same."

Immediately, I snapped, "Get out of here. I am trying to get dressed. Leave me alone!" He walked into another room, mumbling. I shook my head thinking, **What a pest!** But with this new, softer approach, he had planted a seed of doubt.

Later, during my session with Thom, I brought it up. Of course, tattling on Ed was a great recovery tool because acknowledging his influence to someone else took away his power. But then Thom clued me in about Ed's new approach. "He is repeating things to you in a calm, soothing voice to get your attention, hoping that you will believe him. In this case, he is trying to hypnotize you into thinking your left leg is bigger than your right. Here, let me show you."

He instructed me to sit with my feet flat on the floor in

a comfortable position and rest my hands on my lap. Then he told me to close my eyes, relax, and listen. In a calming monotone, he said that my left arm was becoming very heavy—heavier than my right—like a weight against my leg. He was descriptive and soothing at the same time.

After a few minutes, he told me to open my eyes, "How do you feel?"

"Oh my gosh, my left arm feels so heavy!" I answered.

He asked, "Do you really believe your left arm is now heavier than your right?"

"No," I said, "but it feels that way."

Then he explained, "That's the power of hypnosis—and that is what Ed is trying to do to you."

Of course, I realized Thom was right. Ed was trying to convince me of something untrue by being soft and sweet. He tried to trick me! *Who does he think he's playing with? I'll show him!*

The next time he tried to hypnotize me I told him a few times, "Ed, I know what you are trying to do and it won't work. I'm stronger than you." Eventually, he got it and left. And to help me keep him at bay, I went out for lunch and enjoyed my own company!

RECOVERY TOOLS

- Tattleing on Ed
- Talking back to Ed
- Distraction
- Going out to eat
- Talk therapy
- Following a meal plan

REFLECTIONS

Does Ed sneak up on you when you least expect it? Is he trying to hypnotize or trick you? Describe how his voice sounds when he's being sneaky. The next time you feel him trying to manipulate you, tell someone. Don't fight this battle alone!

SECTION 4

THE ESCAPE—
FINDING FREEDOM

73

BEING PRESENT

*"Once I got better at going against what Ed said, I finally had
some peace in my head—space and time to think. I could just let
Ed be background noise and remind myself of his insignificance."*

I had the afternoon to myself for a change—nothing to do,
nowhere to go, no one to see. Of all the things I could have
done—read a book, write, go for a walk—I decided to flip on
the tube and watch one of my favorite shows. I felt that just
being present in the moment and chilling sounded great. So I
tossed off my shoes and got cozy on the sofa.

After awhile, I realized something pretty amazing: I was
actually able to just sit there and watch TV! Where was all the
noise in my head and usual anxiety when I tried to relax? This
was a wonderful, strange occurrence.

Not too long ago I could not "just sit" and look at televi-
sion without my mind racing and Ed talking to me the entire
time. I wasn't able to concentrate on a show and follow what
was going on, because Ed would blabber away that I was wast-
ing my time and needed to do something for him, not me. I
never had a moment's peace as thoughts of food, numbers, and
rules occupied my head. I also had to be multitasking while I
front of the tube—I just couldn't sit still.

Once I got better at rebelling against Ed, I finally had some
peace in my head—space and time to think. I could just let Ed
be background noise and, from time to time, remind myself (and
him!) of his insignificance; he is nobody, nothing! But I could "be"
and "do" anything I wanted because I was learning to be present
and free in the moment. My life was becoming my own.

RECOVERY TOOLS

• Being present

REFLECTIONS

Stop and listen. Sit in a quiet place and just be for five minutes. Close your eyes and focus on your breathing to calm your mind. What do you hear? Take it all in, and then open your eyes. Write down what you heard and how it made you feel.

74

WEIGHT ACCEPTANCE

*"Through recovery I had deepened the trust I had for my body
and realized with absolute certainty that it would not betray
me. I did not have to be so cautious."*

At every appointment, Dr. G. "blind" weighed me, which significantly decreased my anxiety about "the number." I actually didn't know how much I weighed, although I knew that I'd been gaining and wondered if it was too high, too low, or just right. I decided to talk to Dr. G. about it. At our next meeting, as I was getting dressed and she was typing my information into the computer, I asked, "Dr. G., is my weight range the maximum I should ever weigh?" I waited on the other side of the curtain in a panic. As usual, my heart was beating like crazy and my mouth was dry.

Without hesitating she responded, "Um, no Cheryl. It's not."

Ed reacted quickly by saying that Dr. G. only wanted to get me fat and I shouldn't listen to *anything* she had to say. But he'd been telling me this kind of thing all along, and now I knew how to deal with it. I told him to be quiet. Dr. G. was a great doctor, and I trusted her to keep me safe and healthy.

I also reassured myself that it didn't matter what I weighed because through recovery I had deepened the trust I had for my body and realized with absolute certainty that it would not betray me. I did not have to be so cautious. With proper nourishment, my weight would level out at a comfortable, healthy level that was just *right for me*. Despite Ed's protests, I would continue learn different ways to take care of my body and accept that it would find its own best weight.

I continued to avoid Ed's advice and concentrated on healthy behaviors—and at my next appointment with Dr. G. I didn't need to ask anything about "the number." It didn't matter anymore, which I took as a sign of progress—one step closer to accepting my body and loving myself in every moment.

RECOVERY TOOLS

- Acceptance
- Talking back to Ed
- Trust
- Keeping outpatient appointments

REFLECTIONS

When you take care of yourself and nourish your body, its weight naturally ends up where it should. Acceptance of this fact is essential! Write down three positive messages about you and your body (even if you don't fully believe them) and read them daily. You can write these on cards and carry them with you. For example: "I am strong, and my body is a vehicle I trust and love." Reading these messages helps to bring about acceptance.

75

EAT AND ENJOY
A FEAR FOOD

*"I was in charge! I recognized that a treat was something
delicious and decadent—something that enhanced
my life not an opportunity for deprivation."*

While at work one Tuesday morning, my cell phone beeped.
I'd received a text message from my co-worker and longtime
friend, Sharon: "I got you a yummy treat." I immediately guessed
what she might be bringing me—a Boston cream donut!

Ed tried to worm his way in, "No way are you eating that!"
But I hadn't had a donut recently and deserved a treat, especially my favorite one. I continued with the positive self-talk
and reframing until my morning snack time arrived. My recovery voice was dominating the conversation in my head, so Ed
was at bay. Under no circumstances would I allow him to have
the last word. *Never* let Ed have the last word!

Then Sharon walked in with the bag in her hand and—lo
and behold—I was right. She had gotten me Boston cream donut. We sat together at our desks, talking, laughing, and eating
our donuts just like regular folks. I enjoyed every minute and
savored every bite.

Not too long ago Ed would have taken over, and I would
not have eaten that donut. I'd have gone into full-fledged panic
mode, gotten ticked off, and thought of any excuse not to eat
it. But those days were over. I was in charge! I recognized that
a treat was something delicious and decadent—something that
enhanced my life, not an opportunity for deprivation.

I'd come a long way. Not only did I eat the donut and
enjoy it, but Sharon felt comfortable enough to get it for me.

She and I had been friends for 15 years, so she knew all too well the craziness that came along with an eating disorder. In the past, she wouldn't have bought me something so sweet for fear I would yell at her and have an attitude for the rest of the day—all because of Ed. However, with my recovery, she could see how far I had come and was confident that I'd appreciate her kind gesture.

RECOVERY TOOLS

- Eating a fear food
- Positive self-talk
- Talking with supports
- Laughter
- Eating with supports

REFLECTIONS

When was the last time you enjoyed a treat with a friend? Write down five yummy foods that you want to share with a friend, perhaps your favorites or treats you remember from childhood. Call up a friend and plan a time to get together and enjoy them. Remember, there is no such thing as bad food—all food is okay! You deserve it. You are worth it.

76

POSITIVE MANTRA

"I wracked my brain to come up with a successful approach to her loose lips. Eventually, I settled on a mantra, 'I am healthy and happy.' Whatever my friend might say to awaken Ed, I'd be ready with that phrase."

I made plans with a friend I had not seen for many months. We'd known each other for years, so she knew all about my struggles with anorexia. After we set up a time to meet, I knew that I needed to prepare myself, because she had a remarkable knack for innocently saying the wrong thing. She meant no harm, and I loved her, but some of her past statements had disastrous effects. For example, once she told me that my dress made me look heavy, and Ed latched on. I subsequently exercised relentlessly and restricted my food. Back then I paid attention to what he wanted me to do, but no more.

Before our get together, I wracked my brain to come up with a successful approach to her loose lips. Eventually, I settled on a mantra, "I am healthy and happy." Whatever my friend might say to awaken Ed, I'd have that phrase in my pocket.

Finally, the day came and we met at a restaurant. I felt ready, but it was still a surprise when, in the middle of enjoying each other's company, BAM—out it came, "Compared to what you looked liked before, Cheryl, you look overweight!"

As though hit by a sudden blast of wind, I leaned back into the booth, her words rolling around in my head. Almost instantly Ed started in, but I knew just what to do. Over and over I said to myself, "I am not overweight, I am healthy and happy."

I could hear Ed in the background saying, "See, she's

right, she wouldn't lie to you. You're fat! You need to lose some weight, and I can help you do it."

But the sound of the mantra was stronger and gave me the power to respond rationally. She was right and probably meant it as a way to compliment my recovery. In a way, she was being a good friend for noticing how my hard work had paid off. I chuckled and tossed any potential negativity aside.

I understood that people make offhand remarks without thinking about the consequences. I, however, could choose how to react. That time, using my mantra worked perfectly! Not only was I able to eat my meal comfortably, I also ended up having a great time with my friend.

RECOVERY TOOLS

- Positive mantra
- Following a meal plan
- Socializing
- Eating with supports

REFLECTIONS

If a friend that you love and trust said the same statement to you, how would you react? Write three statements to counter those words. Then write a mantra that you could say over and over to yourself for positive reinforcement.

77

REJOIN SOCIETY

"As Ed began to slowly disappear, I spent my time in much healthier ways. My life filled up with fun, friends, and relaxation. I took control of my life's calendar and began to enjoy living each day."

When in the depths of my eating disorder, my social drive was nonexistent. I only wanted to be alone with Ed and away from everything and everyone else. I'd committed myself to him and him alone. So, I stayed isolated.

As my recovery began, though, I slowly came of out isolation and rejoined the world around me. Being in the world again felt like I was exposing myself. The security blanket around me was slowly coming off, and people were looking. I could see them and they could see me. I didn't have Ed to hide behind. I wondered, *Will people like me? Will I be fun to go out with? Can I really do this? Am I a good friend?* Despite being somewhat terrified, I knew deep inside that I had to socialize to move forward.

I found myself doing things I'd never done before. I became much more spontaneous, which was never the case before recovery. I had the energy to do errands, where before, Ed had always drained me. Also, as I've previously mentioned, I conquered my fear of going out to dinner with friends, which became an important part of my life. Gradually I developed the physical and emotional strength to do all kinds of new things and connect with all kinds of people. Recovery gave that to me.

As Ed began to slowly disappear, I spent my time in much healthier ways. Life filled up with fun, friends, relaxation, and so much more. I took control of my life's calendar and began to enjoy living each day. And I showed Ed who's boss—ME!

RECOVERY TOOLS

- Rejoining society
- Socializing
- Going out to eat
- Following a meal plan

REFLECTIONS

Without Ed, life is amazing and has endless possibilities. When you plan your day, who is in control of your calendar? What would an Ed-free day be like for you? Where would you go, what would you do, and how would you nourish yourself? Describe this amazing day in writing. Try living your dream. It's within your reach.

78

ME TIME

"Without Ed, I saw that life could be a kind of therapy because I was constantly learning new lessons. The more I healed, the more time I earned to simply live that life— one I had neglected for years."

At the end of a session with Bob, he had a small smirk on his face, as though he was about to say something important. His words took me by surprise, "You've earned it. I'll see you in two weeks." It took me a minute to realize what he was saying. For many years, I'd gone to individual therapy at least once a week. Suddenly, I was being told I could take a week off!

Dumfounded, I said, "What? I don't have to come back here for *two* weeks?"

He smiled and nodded, "Yes."

I was floored by this amazing, new concept. Honestly, fear overcame me for a moment, because I had been in therapy nonstop for so long. *Would I be okay?* I wanted to snap right back to Bob and say, "No, I'm not ready to take a break." But I realized that he was rewarding me and felt that it was something I needed.

Bob said I had worked so hard and made such great progress that I deserved some extra "Cheryl time" to do new things and have fun. He also reminded me that my free time had already increased because of my recovery. I was no longer obsessing about rules or participating in eating disorder behaviors.

So on my regularly-scheduled therapy night, there I was, sitting in a restaurant and having dinner with friends. (I purposely decided to do that, much to Ed's chagrin.) We were chatting up a storm, laughing so hard our bellies hurt; and, I had the thought, *This sure is more enjoyable than hanging out with Ed, or even doing therapy!*

A few months passed, and I got used to the extra "Cheryl time." Soon enough, Bob said, "I'll see you in three weeks."

I smiled right back at him and without hesitation answered, "Three weeks, great, I'll see you then!"

As I got further along in recovery, my appointments got further and further apart. Without Ed, I saw that life was actually a kind of therapy, because I was constantly learning new lessons. The more I healed, the more time I learned to simply live that life—one I had neglected for years.

RECOVERY TOOLS

- Taking "me time"
- Talk therapy
- Going out to eat
- Eating with supports
- Socializing
- Fun
- Laughter

REFLECTIONS

As you move forward in recovery and further away from Ed, you will earn free time. How would you most like to fill your "me time?" Will you go to dinner with friends? Go to the movies? Go shopping? List five things you would like to do (without Ed), then, pull out your list and begin to cross them off one by one!

79

SELF-ACCEPTANCE

"It took me a minute to wrap my brain around what he was saying, but I came to the realization that I was already perfectly fine. I'd been searching for something that I had all along."

My birthday was coming up and I decided to celebrate my transformed life by doing something to show off the new me. I wanted people to see on the outside what I was finally feeling on the inside. I came up with the perfect idea: a makeover in New York City. I'd always dreamed of getting my hair done in a famous salon, and my birthday would be the perfect opportunity.

When the big day came, I couldn't contain my excitement. The Big Apple! The salon was beautiful—silver and blue with multiple levels. Cappuccinos were being passed around, and stylists, colorists, and manicurists—all dressed in black pants and white shirts—were waiting on clients' every need. All the chairs in the salon were full.

My colorist, Clark, ran his fingers through my hair. "Nice color," he said. "Let's do a gloss and a few highlights, but keep the brown." I was a little disappointed to be staying with same color, but he was the expert.

Then Robert, my hairstylist, came over, and asked me a few questions. I explained that I was open to change and a new look. He played with my hair and suggested cutting a bit off the back and styling the sides.

I said, "Great, let's get started."

As I sat in his chair, my heart beat with excitement. I

couldn't wait to see what they would do and how I would look. Clark started with the coloring, and then I moved on to Robert. He combed out my hair and began cutting a little bit here and there, but after a few minutes said, "I've changed my mind. I'm going to texture your hair and leave the bulk of it the way it is." Again I felt a pang of disappointment, but said, "Okay, you're the expert."

Finally, after the blow-drying and brushing were completed, I was ready for the final outcome! My belly did flips as Robert turned the chair around to face the mirror. To my surprise, I looked exactly the same!

I said an appropriate "thank you," but my heart wasn't in it. *I came all this way for this?* My friend who came with me raved and said it seemed a lot different, but I knew she was just being nice. I'd hoped for the wow factor and didn't get it.

The next day during a session with Thom, I described my birthday disappointment, and after listening to my story, he said, "Cheryl, you already had what you were seeking. Nothing needs to change. You already look like you need to look."

It took me a minute to wrap my brain around what he was saying, but he was right—I was already perfectly fine. I'd been searching for something that I had all along, and that outcome was far more profound than a haircut!

When I went into work on Monday morning, my friends said, "You don't look any different. What happened to the makeover?"

"Apparently, I'm fine just the way I am," I replied.

To which someone responded, "We could have told you that!"

My birthday gift ended up being far greater than what I'd imagined getting. That lesson in self-acceptance was the best present I could have had, and I will keep it forever!

RECOVERY TOOLS

- Self-acceptance
- Friends
- Self-care
- Talk therapy

REFLECTIONS

We tend to go through life only looking at ourselves from the outside. Sit in a quiet place and look at yourself from the inside out. What do you see? What do you feel? Write down five positive words that describe you and read them out loud. Are you loyal, honest, friendly, compassionate? In the end, *you* are the best gift you can give yourself.

80

LIVE BY A
HEALTHY RULE

*"Feelings of accomplishment, strength, and courage ran
through my body. At one time I had needed to be saved,
and by leaving Ed and following recovery, I could now
help save someone else's life."*

As I mentioned in a previous chapter ("Transforming Ed's
Rules"), one of Ed's rules was that I not be allowed to weigh
enough to give blood. He told me that if my weight climbed
that high, I was a failure and a disappointment to him. Through
recovery, though, I have learned how to recognize and transform his rules…and live by my new ones.

One day while driving home from work, I saw a sign for
a blood drive. Of course, Ed's rule came to mind, but as I
drove down the street, I knew what I had to do and why. I was
healthy enough to donate and that by taking care of myself and
going against Ed, I now had the ability to help others in this
positive way.

When I checked in at the front table, Ed whispered,
"Cheryl, if they let you do this, it means you are fat."

I rolled my eyes, shook my head in disgust and said,
"Whatever." I knew he was lying.

I filled out the paperwork, answered the questions, had
the necessary tests, and was on my way. My chest expanded
with pride because I knew how far I had come to get there.
When the nurse stuck me with the needle, I envisioned it jab-
bing Ed and said to myself, *Hey Ed, how does that feel?* I smiled
with the knowledge that I was sticking it to him!

As I lay there with the blood bag attached to my arm, feelings of accomplishment, strength, and courage ran through my body. At one time I had needed to be saved, and by leaving Ed and following recovery, I could now help save someone else's life. No one else in that room knew about the pain and struggle I had to go through to get there that day, but I did!

That blood drive was my first, but it would not be my last.

RECOVERY TOOLS

- Living by a healthy rule
- Talking back to Ed
- Volunteering

REFLECTIONS

Empower yourself by doing things Ed had said were forbidden. That will show Ed who is boss and who is in control—YOU. What will one of your firsts be? List five things that Ed has said you can't do, and then show him you mean business by doing them. Feel the power behind your actions.

81

ACCEPTING COMPLIMENTS

"I had developed the skill to keep Ed quiet. Finally, I could hear someone's flattery and accept it with an open heart. I'd worked hard in my recovery and was thrilled that it showed from the inside out."

The week was coming to an end, and talk around the office centered around everybody's weekend plans. As I sat at my desk engrossed in my job, I heard someone nearby bustling around, but wasn't paying attention to who was there.

After a few minutes I looked up to see Lou, who had been taking care of our office plants on a weekly basis for many years. As usual, he stopped by my desk and we chatted a bit. This time, while he talked to me, his head tilted sideways, his eyebrows went up, and a grin came over his face.

"Is everything okay?" I asked.

"I am just noticing something," he replied. I looked at him inquisitively. "I have to say, Cheryl—you just look so healthy and vibrant!"

His compliment came from out of the blue, and I quietly thanked him. Lou had no idea about my struggles with Ed, but his words were genuine and meant a lot to me. Had he said the same thing several months earlier, I'd have recoiled. Ed would have told me that I had let myself go. He always said that healthy equaled fat, which was nothing but a lie.

I had developed the skill to keep Ed quiet. Finally, I could hear someone's flattery and accept it with an open heart. Lou's words (and his noticing) were icing on the cake. I'd worked hard in my recovery and was thrilled that it showed from the inside out.

RECOVERY TOOLS

- Hearing and accepting compliments
- Socializing

REFLECTIONS

Hearing and accepting people's kind words helps you realize who you are and how hard you have worked at recovery. Ask a trusted support to sit with you and give you compliments—all the things they love about you. While you listen, accept what they say, and thank them wholeheartedly. Afterward, write down what they told you and keep it close to you for a reality reminder.

82

RECOVERY REFLECTIONS

"Life was out there for the taking. I had gained the ability and confidence to know that the world held endless possibilities for me, just as it did for that divine baby."

One night I babysat for my friends' daughter, Gabriella, who was three months old. Since I don't have children, I was particularly excited to spend that time with her. I love kids!

Gabriella and I did some baby exercises together and then we played with her toys. After all that activity, she got fussy—her way of announcing that it was dinnertime. I prepared a bottle and sat down to feed her. While she drank, I gazed at her cute, little body. With arms and legs spread eagle and her belly extended and relaxed, she was clearly enjoying her dinner.

As she lay there, I thought about how lucky I was—healthy enough to be trusted to care for such a beautiful being. This would not have been the case when Ed had control over me. People had been afraid of my fragility and lack of concentration, and I couldn't blame them. The thought of even trying to baby-sit when I was so sick gave me chills down my spine, because something bad could have happened in a split second. However, with recovery came the strength, attentiveness, and willingness to be responsible not only for my own life, but for the life of another being.

I also reflected about how Gabriella was so comfortable in her body, without a care in the world or any self-judgment. By contrast, since I'd been young, I'd gone through years of hating my body and being critical of everything about me. Of course, that was all Ed's doing. Seeing Gabriella just being in the moment gave me hope, and I wondered, *why can't I be free like that? What's stopping me?* I realized the answer was "nothing."

I also thought about how Gabriella's parents put their trust in me, and how I had to learn to trust my treatment team and myself. I felt eternally grateful that my hard work could give me such a wonderful gift.

Gabriella was so innocent and alive, and being with her reminded me that life was out there for the taking. I had gained the ability and confidence to know that the world held endless possibilities for me, just as it did for that beautiful baby.

RECOVERY TOOLS

- Reflection

REFLECTIONS

Look back through your recovery process. What vision has recovery given you? What have you noticed is different now than it was before? Make a list of gifts that recovery has given to you. You'll be surprised by how many things you will come up with.

83

GIVE BACK

"When I was with Ed, my life was empty, lacking self-love or the ability to look outside of myself. Now that I have found recovery, happiness follows me everywhere, blessing me with the strength to give back."

When I was listening to Ed, I had limited ability to be there for anyone else—I could barely help myself! Fortunately, I found the hope and help I needed and created a better life. Today I share my triumphant story through this book and speaking engagements, but have also been blessed to do even more.

My friend, Shannon Cutts, is the author of *Beating Ana: How to Outsmart Your Eating Disorder and Take Your Life Back* and founder of Key-to-Life and MentorCONNECT (*www.mentorconnect-Ed.org*), a program that connects people who need eating disorder recovery support ("mentees") with those who can offer it ("mentors"). I had the time and ability to give so, I spoke with Shannon about getting involved and she signed me up to become a volunteer mentor.

I took on two mentees and talked to them daily. We'd brainstorm ways to keep them in the recovery mindset, and they looked to me for guidance and suggestions in their fight against Ed. We'd talk about daily struggles, fears, recovery tools, and visions for the future. I became their confidante and let them know that they were not alone. They gained a connection to someone who understood their pain and struggles and who had made it through to the other side to achieve lasting recovery.

These relationships also helped *me* by reminding me how far I had come and strengthening my resolve to stay healthy.

It saddened me to hear their despair, because I wanted to take their pain away, while knowing I couldn't. Recovery is a process—one that must be gone through step-by-step, and I continually told them that—in the end—it's all worth it.

I've also been fortunate to help out at Thom's "Beyond Eating Disorders" weekend retreats in Tennessee (*www.nutshellwisdom.com*). A few months after my sessions with him ended, he called to tell me how impressed he was with my hard work in recovery and that he loved my ability and passion to reach out to others. The next moment took my breath away, because he invited me to work with him! My eyes filled with tears of pride and I felt truly honored. I *never* thought that I would go from being a participant at one of his retreats to working at them. These weekends are filled with hope, strength, love, determination, fun, respect, and support for anyone in recovery from an eating disorder.

Being able to help others who are struggling makes me happy and gives me a sense of purpose. When I was with Ed, my life was empty, lacking self-love or the capacity to look outside of myself. Now that I have found recovery, happiness follows me everywhere, blessing me with the strength to give back.

RECOVERY TOOLS

- Sharing recovery knowledge (give back)
- Mentoring
- Workshops

REFLECTIONS

Recovery gives you strength and knowledge. Are you ready, strong enough, and willing to assist others? List three ways that you might give support and how it would help you in your own recovery.

84

CREATE & REDISCOVER FOOD TRADITIONS

"Because of recovery, I can welcome new food traditions or reconnect with old ones and realize that they are all a normal part of healthy living."

I've always been a Boston Red Sox fan and have attended many games over the years. Fenway Park is a great place to bring the family to see a game. Recently I've been fortunate enough to take along my niece, Stephanie.

One day at the park, while we were walking around watching batting practice and checking out the sights, we came upon a concession stand.

I pointed it out and impulsively said, "Oh my gosh, I love fried dough."

"Me too!" she replied.

I promised Stephanie that we would get some, and during the fifth inning, we looked at each other and both exclaimed, "Fried dough!" We marched over to the stand and ordered. We put on toppings, took a few bites, and headed back our seats. It was so good!

A few weeks later, on the way to another game together, we were reminiscing and remembered the mouthwatering dessert and the fun we had had. So, in the fifth inning we looked at each other and said in unison, "Fried dough!" We marched down to the stand, placed our order, and took a few bites—just like before and just as yummy.

The next time we went to a game together, we looked at each other during the fifth inning and off we went! On our way to the stand, Stephanie said, "Auntie, this is becoming our new tradition."

"Stephanie, you are exactly right," I laughed. "Let's call it Fried Dough at Fenway!" And a tradition was indeed born—and a delicious one at that!

Before recovery, Ed would have never even let me think about something so decadent, let alone say out loud that I loved it! He'd have berated me about getting too fat and would have told me I was weak if I took even one bite.

Today, recovery squashes Ed's voice even before he can get a word out. I stay in the moment and can enjoy eating something new and different—no guilt allowed. I know that Stephanie and I are making memories together. Ed cannot and will not ever take that away from me again; I won't let him.

Traditions around food are a normal part of human culture. Because of recovery, I can welcome new ones or reconnect with old ones, knowing they are they are all a normal part of healthy living.

RECOVERY TOOLS

- Creating/rediscovering food traditions
- Family
- Fun activities
- Laughter
- Eating with supports

REFLECTIONS

What are some traditions that you once enjoyed? How does Ed stand in your way of participating in those or forming new ones? Write down three ways that you can push Ed aside and get back to those traditions that you love—and also make new ones.

85

ATTEND RECOVERY EVENTS

"I was proof that their dedication to serving others changed lives and I glowed with a sense of accomplishment and pride. All my hard work had paid off."

My local eating disorder association, Multi-Service Eating Disorders Association (*www.medainc.org*), holds an annual fundraising gala. One year they honored my doctor, Dr. Suzanne Gleysteen. Without hesitation, I knew I wanted to be there to thank her for everything she had done for me and to tell her how much I loved and respected her.

I was nervous and excited, because I expected that many of the healthcare providers who had worked with me would be there. Seeing them in a social setting would be interesting. *Would any of them even remember me?* On the day of the benefit, I had my hair and makeup done, and—I must admit—my evening gown looked great on me!

Rachel and I arrived at the gala and entered a room filled with over 200 mingling people. Quickly, we were met with familiar faces. After catching up, we roamed around as one does at such events.

I soon spotted Dr. Gleysteen and walked up to congratulate her and express my appreciation. She looked beautiful and happy and thanked us for being there. Next I saw Bob, and we exchanged greetings, as well. As I looked around, I recognized several other people who had helped with my recovery, and to my pleasant surprise, most of them remembered me. I felt grateful to have the opportunity to tell them how much their support had meant. I also think they enjoyed getting an update on my recovery, because oftentimes they devote themselves to their patients without ever knowing what happens to us after we leave treatment.

During dinner, various speakers addressed the guests with great passion, which made the atmosphere incredibly nourishing. Finally, Dr. Gleysteen received a grand introduction, and before she even said a word, the entire audience gave her a standing ovation. The gratitude in the room was exhilarating and electric. When she spoke, my heart filled with tremendous admiration and appreciation for her. The work she has done to help people recover from eating disorders is extraordinary.

For me, the whole evening represented a kind of homecoming—a personal celebration of sorts. There I was, a survivor in a room filled with people who care and, specifically, individuals who helped me become free from Ed. I was proof that their dedication to serving others changed lives, and I glowed with a sense of accomplishment and pride. All my hard work had paid off. Thanks in large part to the people in that room and others like them, I did it!

RECOVERY TOOLS

- Attending recovery events
- Socializing
- Eating with supports

REFLECTIONS

What fills you with a sense of pride? Is it eating a fear food, being able to communicate, or seeking treatment? Think about yourself and your recovery, and list three things that fill you with pride. Also, attend fundraising benefits, recovery workshops, and other events that bring together people dedicated to overcoming eating disorders.

86

GIVE THANKS

"Now on Thanksgiving Day—and every day—I give thanks for my recovery and for the fact that I am alive to enjoy each moment."

I woke up on Thanksgiving Day with excitement running through my veins. I was looking forward to spending the day with my family, especially my niece and nephew. With Tupperware in hand for leftovers, I arrived at my parents' house just after noon.

We gathered in a warm home with love in the air. The aroma of turkey and Mom's stuffing filled the house. We chatted about daily life and the upcoming Christmas season while we waited for the dinner bell to ring. Then we sat down to a hot meal with family gathered around the table. Laughter filled the room. While we ate, we caught up on family gossip and reminisced about the old days. We finished dinner, cleaned up, and moved to the living room to relax.

My nephew asked me, "Auntie Cheryl, will you play checkers with me?"

"Of course I will," I answered.

We played and belly laughed for half an hour. It was great to see him sitting across from me smiling, laughing, and enjoying himself. He legitimately beat me a few times, too! These moments with him were precious to me, because I was spending quality time with family and making memories. I wasn't beating myself up over what I ate or using a negative behavior to get through a feeling. I was relaxed, being in the now, and enjoying it. This is what Thanksgiving is all about—family, friends, and loving memories, not food.

There had been a time when Thanksgiving Day had brought me nothing but anxiety, stress, and fear. I feared seeing the food, feared eating it, and dreaded having to see everyone. From Thanksgiving to New Year's I was one big anxiety-filled ball, from which I could not break free. I obsessed about everything—calories, food, parties, people, and presents. You name it—I obsessed about it. My brain did not get a moment's peace. It was constantly on the go.

After recovery, though, the holidays held a different meaning for me. I found that I could enjoy myself and let food take the back seat. The company I kept and the memories I made were more important to me—and Ed was not invited. The food was literally just filler.

Now on Thanksgiving Day—and every day—I give thanks for my recovery and for the fact that I am alive to enjoy each moment.

RECOVERY TOOLS

- Giving thanks
- Following a meal plan
- Playing games
- Laughter
- Family
- Eating with supports

REFLECTIONS

At Thanksgiving, we reflect on things that we are thankful for, like family, friends, good health, or a good job. Being in recovery allows you to see and appreciate things you never could before because Ed was in the way. Push Ed aside right now and list five things that you are thankful for. To keep the positive recovery momentum going, keep a gratitude journal and list five things that you are thankful for each night.

87

SOCIALIZING

"Being with friends, loving and accepting myself, having fun, and trying new things are some of the experiences that recovery showed me. I didn't fear them any longer; I appreciated and welcomed them all."

It was a date: Friday would be girls' night out. I was excited. In the old days, this kind of thing didn't happen. Isolation was more like it. Ed used to tell me that I only needed him, and silly me believed him. Now I could hang out with friends whenever I wanted.

What's more, we were going to meet at a restaurant I had never been to before, and I was excited about it. In the old days, I hardly ever ventured out to a restaurant, much less a new one with unfamiliar menus and meals. These days, with so much recovery work under my belt, I could go wherever I wanted.

So after work on Friday I went home, took care of the dogs, and freshened up a bit before leaving. I put on my new black jeans, a red shirt, and black boots. I felt good about myself and looked in the mirror before I left.

"Damn, I look good!" I said, which was a statement that Ed never let me say. He used to pick me apart piece by piece until I ended up crying and feeling horrible about myself. Not anymore. At this point I could honestly see that I *did* look good— and what's more important, I *felt* good, too!

I pulled into the lot, found a space, and parked the car. It was cold outside and the wind was blowing, so I hurried to the door. I was so excited to see everyone sitting there in the lobby.

"Hey, girls," I said, as we exchanged hugs and hellos. Then the hostess led us to a round table in the corner of the room—a perfect place to chat and catch up. We were all talking and joking when she handed us menus and told us the specials so we could decide what to eat. Even this was a big change for me! Recovery has given me the ability to look at a menu and engage in conversations with friends at the same time. Before, I would have been engrossed in thoughts and fears about the food, calories, portion size, wondering what others would be getting, and so on. Now, I was able to look and talk at the same time without anxiety.

I also couldn't wait to try something new, because, during recovery, I had made it a point to try different dishes to expand my food horizons and avoid the trap of safety foods. After much practice, I could walk into any restaurant (or friend's home) and eat without panic, fear, rules, guilt, or judgment. After a few minutes, the waitress came and took our order. I couldn't wait to dig in!

Our girls' night out continued with laugh after laugh. At times we were so loud that the other patrons stared at us—but we didn't care! It was great to see each other and be together. Being with friends, loving and accepting myself, having fun, and trying new things are some of the experiences that recovery showed me. I didn't fear them any longer; I appreciated and welcomed them all.

RECOVERY TOOLS

- Socializing
- Positive self-talk
- Going out to eat
- Following a meal plan
- Laughter
- Eating new foods
- Friends
- Eating with supports

Going out with friends is a normal activity that is fun and enjoyable. Is there anything you didn't get a chance to do that you would like because Ed stood in your way? What steps could you take to push Ed aside? What would you do differently next time?

88

SUPPORT

"Throughout my recovery, whenever I had asked, or the situation had called for it, my friends, family, treatment team (and even strangers in the bleachers!) had given me the courage, guidance, and strength to keep going."

I went to Club Med in Mexico on vacation and discovered they have a circus school there—with a trapeze. I sat on the bleachers one day, in ninety-degree heat with the sun blazing down, and watched other people climb up and over to the platform, jump off, and go. I'm deathly afraid of heights, but I have always wanted to do that. Unsure whether I would have the guts, I made a snap decision and decided to go for it.

Armed with instructions from the trainer, I knew only the basic dos and don'ts of flying. My stomach was doing flips. I wasn't sure if the beads of sweat on my brow were from the sun or from my nerves!

Saying my good-byes to the folks on the ground, I began climbing up the wobbly, two-feet wide, four-story ladder. On the way up, I looked straight ahead so I could keep my eyes on the ocean beyond; I figured it would help me be less afraid if I could see something so beautiful. Well, it didn't work so well! Fear washed over me as I stopped mid-climb and said out loud, "I can't do this. I'm scared." Friends down below and the other people there cheered me on, sending positive thoughts my way. "You can do it, Cheryl!" they shouted. "Just put one foot in front of the other and climb."

But I was paralyzed. *Should I continue up or get down?* As I stood there and pondered that question, the voice of Recovery actually stepped in and said, "Cheryl, you found the strength inside of you to fight off Ed, so climbing this ladder will be a breeze. You can do it."

So I said to myself, "I *can* totally do this. I am in recovery; and in recovery I can do anything." And so I did. One step at a time, I reached the top. Then I found my footing, grabbed that trapeze, and flew through the air. It was so much fun.

This time, as was the case so many times in recent months, I had the just the right kind of support and encouragement I needed to reach my goal. In fact, throughout my recovery, whenever I had asked, or the situation had called for it, my friends, family, treatment team (and even strangers in the bleachers!) had given me the courage, guidance, and strength to keep going. Without them, I would not have been able to put one foot in front of the other and climb to the top.

RECOVERY TOOLS

- Support people
- Positive self-talk
- Listen for/to Recovery
- Friends
- Taking risks

REFLECTIONS

Overcoming fears makes us stronger in life and in our recovery by giving us the ability to see how far we have come, what we have accomplished, and how hard we have worked. Make a list of fears that have you overcome in your recovery. Are there more you want to overcome? List those as well and then add the steps you can take to overcome them. You can do it…one step at a time!

AFTERWORD

With life come ups and downs, twists and turns, feelings and stressors, and so much more. How we react and what we do to help us get through it all is key. When we come up against challenges every single day, the only option to keep us safe and on the right path is to follow recovery. In doing so, we remain healthy and strong to continue the fight and win. With recovery we can face anything and conquer all.

Not that long ago, life threw me a devastating curve ball. I was lying in bed, relaxed and cozy, talking with my wife, Rachel, when she informed me she wanted a divorce. Her words ripped open my heart. *How can this be happening to me? We have a family and built a life together.* In a split second, my life as I knew it had changed forever.

The months that followed were extremely painful and filled with the on-goings of divorce: mediation, the division of assets, selling our home, a court date, and goodbyes. The reality of losing my best friend and confidant, my two dogs, my home, my safety and security, our future hopes and dreams seemed completely unbearable. Every day, I was filled with intense feelings of grief, fear, and hurt.

Yet, despite the fact that I lost many pieces of my life that had made me feel whole, the most important thing I didn't lose was my recovery. I kept it close by my side the entire time. I would often think back to my life with Ed and the old ways I coped and would shudder at the thought. I knew that going down that road again wouldn't take any of the pain away—it would only give me more. So, I focused on my gratitude for what I had accomplished and how far I had come. And no matter how bad it got, I never let go of recovery; during those most difficult times, I held on even tighter.

I continued to follow recovery each day, using a lot of tools in this book to help me through my darkest days. I wasn't going to let anything take all the hard work I had done away from me! I found particular comfort (and said them daily) in a few lines from the song "A Little Bit Stronger" by Sara Evans, "I know my heart will never be the same, but I'm telling myself I'll be ok. Even on my weakest days, I get a little bit stronger."

Life goes on and so does my recovery, because for me it is all a journey, not a destination—and I honor, celebrate, and respect every minute of it. I learn more about myself each day and welcome with open arms every feeling and emotion that goes along with it. I can now say that I am in control of my life; there are no rules, no guilt, no despair or shame—just freedom, honesty, joy, and beauty. I am in control of my reactions, my world, and my destiny. I am finally free; Ed has been silenced.

Recovery can be yours. You have the power of will and the choice to break free. With recovery, it all gets better: You begin to heal from the inside out and truly see who you are without Ed's influence.

Remember this: Ed takes and Recovery gives.

My hope for you is that you will find the light that is inside of you and use it to guide your way to freedom. Take what you like from the pages you've read, weave it into your own recovery process, and see what grows. Show Ed that *you* are the boss—and tell him you don't need him any more. *Tell Ed No!* You *can* do this. You have the strength. If I can do it, you can too.

Recovery is waiting for you. Reach out, take it by the hand, and see where it leads you. You will be amazed at all the places you will go.

ACKNOWLEDGEMENTS

The road in writing this book has been long and winding, but the journey has been fruitful and exciting. Like my recovery, I was not alone in writing this book. I had many friends and family supporting me with every word I typed. I was fortunate to have guidance that was backed by love and friendship, without which this book would not have been be possible. I am deeply grateful for each one of you and thank you from the depths of my soul. You all have a piece of my heart.

To Dad, Mom, Peter, Stacey, Stephanie, and Stephen: You have been with me through my pain and suffering and then my rebirth. Thank you for your support, love, and guidance in life, my recovery, and in writing this book. Thanks for always being there every time I turned around. I love you all very much.

To Lindsey Hall and Leigh Cohn and the rest of the Gürze team: Thank you for believing and having faith in me and my journey. You respected my voice and never lost sight of my vision. You enhanced my story with your guidance, wisdom, and knowledge all while holding it close to your heart. You are amazing, loving people and I am honored to call you friends. With much love and respect.

To Bob Bordonaro: You were there for me the day my recovery began (and still are), giving me guidance, hope, and strength. With all the falls my recovery brought, you were always there to pick me up and help me get back on track. With tough love and kind words, you never left my side. Thank you for holding my hand on this journey. With love, I am forever grateful.

To the staff at Walden Behavioral Care, thank you for helping "me see me" and giving me the strength and guidance to stand on my own. Your care and presence gave me hope and the ability to take that most important first step towards freedom. I will always hold each of you close to my heart. With deep gratitude and love.

To Dr. Suzanne Gleysteen: Your wit, care, and determination in guiding me through this journey to recovery is respected and honored. I am proud to be your patient. Thank you for being there for me way back when and never losing faith in me. Your support and presence means a lot. With love and admiration.

To Thom Rutledge, the man who showed me the truth about Ed and helped me realize I am separate from him, I am strong, and I don't need Ed to live: From the day I met you, my heart told me you were a special man—and it was right. You challenged, directed, and respected me throughout my entire journey and because of that, I have found freedom. With deep gratitude, awe, and much love.

To Amy Aubertin: Thank you for teaching me to respect, trust, and love something that was once so dreaded and feared. Thanks to you I am not afraid anymore; food is now my friend. With respect and love.

To Dr. Daniel Mollod: Your attentiveness and care in listening to my prescription concerns brought me to a place where I could accept help in various forms and be okay with it. Thank you for guiding me and giving me the ability to feel and experience all that life has to offer. With love and respect.

To all my reviewers: Thank you for your words of support and encouragement in helping me put my best foot forward. You are appreciated.

To all my friends who listened to me rant day in and day out about this book and who never once told me to shut up! You always told me you were proud! Thank you for standing by me in my time of need, showing me love, and helping guide me in the right direction. I love you all.

ABOUT THE AUTHOR

Cheryl Kerrigan is an eating disorder survivor, activist, and contributor to multiple eating disorder recovery books. She is on the Leadership Board (and a mentor) of MentorCONNECT, the first global eating disorder mentoring community and also works with Thom Rutledge at his "Beyond Eating Disorders" recovery retreats. Cheryl "brings recovery to life" by speaking about her experiences at treatment centers and schools around the country and through her blog at *www.getridofed.blogspot.com*. She lives in Woburn, Massachusetts.

Learn more at *www.tellingedno.com* and *www.cherylkerrigan.com*.

ORDER ADDITIONAL COPIES AT BULIMIA.COM

Telling Ed No! is available through most booksellers or may be ordered directly from the Gürze Books website, *bulimia.com,* or by phone at (800)756-7533.

FREE CATALOGUE

The Eating Disorders Resource Catalogue features books and articles on eating and weight-related topics, including body image, size acceptance, self-esteem and more. It also includes listings of nonprofit associations and treatment facilities and is handed out by therapists, educators, and other health care professionals around the world.

BULIMIA.COM

Visit our website for additional resources, including many free articles, hundreds of books, and links to organizations, treatment facilities and other websites.

EATINGDISORDERSBLOGS.COM

EatingDisordersBlogs.com is a website with more than 20 blogs for connecting with others about food and feelings, healthy eating, family concerns, and recovery issues.

Gürze Books has specialized in eating disorders publications and education since 1980.